MY GRANDMOTHER RACHEL

The author aged three.

MY GRANDMOTHER RACHEL

THE STORY OF
WINDSOR'S JEWISH COMMUNITY
1940-1950

Clare Newton

COUNTRY BOOKS

Published by:
Country Books
Courtyard Cottage, Little Longstone, Bakewell, Derbyshire DE45 1NN

ISBN 1 898941 64 5

British Library in Cataloguing in Publication Data:
a catalogue record for this book is available from the British Library.

DEDICATION

This book is dedicated to my yet unborn grandchildren,
my family and to Betty, my beloved cousin,
who was there most of the time.

CONTENTS

INTRODUCTION

At the beginning of World War II hundreds of Jewish people had fled the bombing and landed bag and baggage in the Royal Borough of Windsor. They were a motley crowd with little more than they stood up in with just one thought in mind – to get away from the London blitz. Throughout their history Jews had lived with a packed suitcase in the hall ready to flee, so this was no exception.

Some, of course, had more than the others but none could be considered the Windsor branch of the Rothchilds!

The east end of London was catching most of the blitz and as this was largely a Jewish area they evacuated themselves to places less targetted by the Luftaffe. It was rumoured at the time that Hitler wanted to eat his Christmas dinner in Windsor Castle so it would not be bombed. It never was bombed so maybe the rumour was correct. Only two bombs fell on Windsor during the whole period of the war.

The Jewish influx to the royal borough must have been quite a shock to the indigenous residents. At that time Windsor was a fairly quiet royal town, not geared to hoards of tourists as it is today. The King and Queen were not aware they were there as when I wrote to the Queen Mother in 2001 she said there was so much movement of people at that time that their Majesties were not always made aware of exactly who was where.

This is the story of those Jewish people and my family in particular. The 'Boba' in the book is my grandmother. The Yiddish name for grandmother is Boba and that is what I called her. If there is a heroine in this book it is her, but all the people were giants in their own way.

As far as I know the history of these families has not been charted before so I felt that this situation should be rectified.

IN THE BEGINNING

"Please let me be asleep when they bring the body back. Please, please let me be asleep when they bring the body back", I had heard the policeman at the front door saying that my mother had died in Old Windsor Hospital and they would be bringing the body back.

At the time I was awake in my make-shift bed of two armchairs in the lodger's room. From about two years old I had slept in the front room with the lodger who was a fine lady but a drunk. There was nowhere else in the house for me to sleep.

It was 1944 and my father had been killed that year in Italy. He had been a gunner with the Royal Artillery moving northwards towards Florence. My mother could not live without her love so when she got pneumonia she was quite glad to let the illness take her. I was six years old.

Outside the room I could hear the screams of my grandmother and the aunts who had descended from London to Windsor when the bombs started dropping. The poor policeman must have been horrified at the reaction as he was used to taking bad messages to genteel Windsor folk. These strange Jews who had arrived at the beginning of the war were a queer lot and had no sense of decorum.

The house central to the story, Barry Avenue, Windsor.

Mrs Alice Turner, the lodger, was awake, having been disturbed by the noises in the hall. She was more or less sober as she had slept off most of the previous night's rich ruby wine,

At this time Mrs Turner was about 60 and had henna assisted red hair which she always put in curlers at night however drunk she might be. She also went to bed in her 'air-raid' dress and a row of pearls. This was because she would be respectable if we had to go to the air-raid shelter across the road. The fact that she was drunk half the day didn't obscure the fact that she was a lady.

She was my friend and I loved her with an uncritical love. Her room was a haven of Englishness amidst the hubble bubble of the Jewish world outside her door. The room was a mass of furniture, but it was my haven and warm, and every

12

object meant something to her and consequently to me. Everything was always in its place from the bottle of calamine lotion for her chilblains to the night potty under the bed.

The potty was placed before use in a bag made from the local paper and sewn up two sides, so consequently local papers have an added dimension for me. It was strange that later in my life I should work for the very paper that had lent itself to such an unusual use. I never told the editor to what use his cherished paper had been dedicated.

My mother, grandmother and a various assortment of relatives lived beyond the 'baize' door. Mrs. Turner came from the illegitimate line of George IV and had gone to boarding school by the sea because she had 'throats'. I always thought 'throats' meant that she had many of such things and accepted quite happily that people who had 'throats' went to the sea-side. It was a great disappointment to my child's mind that I had only been blessed with one. When the plural throats diminished to one this was put to great use swallowing gin and rich ruby wine in vast quantities.

I didn't cry when I heard the policeman as his news really didn't hit me as my mother was just another person amongst the others in the house. It was the thought of a 'body' that frightened me, not whose body it was.

Nobody came in to see me as they were all busy with their own inflated emotions. Mrs Turner came over to my bed and suggested we played a game to get back to sleep. She didn't try to explain what had happened as I think she realised that I didn't want the reality explained. That was too much for my tender years.

Every night as we lay in our beds, we would play verbal games. I learnt the alphabet by reciting "I know a girl called Annie, who lives in Acton and who likes apples" followed by "I know a boy called Anthony who lives in Andover and likes apricots". This went on right through the alphabet and we would always laugh like mad when we couldn't think of anything Xerxes would like and where he would live.

When we finished that we would sing songs from the 1930's shows. I used to love the cobbler's song from Chu Chin Chow and 'We'll gather lilacs' from something or other.

From her bed and through a red mist of alcohol Mrs Turner would tell me stories of her boarding school days and when she was a young lady employed by Barkers in Kensington. It was all such a different world to the one I lived in and gave me a vivid picture of life in London just after the First War.

Now with my mother just dead we sang 'Love is a reason for Living' and 'You are my heart's delight' and I fell asleep unaware that my life had changed for ever and that now I was an orphan.

ANOTHER SUITCASE, ANOTHER HALL

Richard the Lionheart and Oliver Cromwell had their Jews and so did George VI, though not in the same way, as he was not aware of their habitation sheltering at the foot of Windsor Castle's walls.

King Richard kept the Jews in England to finance his various adventures to the Holy Land and Oliver Cromwell thought the world would be perfect if all the Jews converted to Christianity. I wonder if it ever crossed Richard's mind that he was using Jewish money to try and Christianise their ancient homeland? George's 'Jews' in Windsor had very little money and certainly none to lend.

At the beginning of World War II dozens of Jewish families had fled the bombing and landed bag and baggage in the royal borough of Windsor. They were a motley crowd with little more than they stood up in with just one thought in mind – to get away from the London blitz. Throughout their history Jews had lived with a packed suitcase in the hall ready to flee persecution of one sort or another, so this was no exception.

The east end of London was catching most of the blitz and as this was largely a Jewish area they evacuated themselves to places less targetted by the Luftwaffe. It was rumoured at the time that Hitler wanted to eat his Christmas dinner in Windsor Castle so it would not be bombed. It never was bombed so maybe the rumour was correct.

Windsor was also a short distance from London and many of the older husbands commuted daily on the workmen's trains to their jobs while the buildings still survived. Many got jobs in Windsor, but, of course, most of the husbands were in the forces.

In September 1939 a group of girls and boys from Stepney Green School, East London, left by tube and train to arrive as evacuees in Windsor. The head teacher, Miss Kate Rose, and several other teachers accompanied the children.

The poor parents had no idea when the children would be leaving London. Every morning they had to go to school ready to leave with haversacks containing a few clothes and shoes. Come the morning of the big day the parents were only told later that their children had actually left and gone off to Windsor.

On the children's arrival they were taken to a junior school on Bachelor's Acre, just behind the castle, and given some biscuits and a tin of corned beef. The upheaval for these poor children must have been horrendous, suddenly plucked from their homes and school and landing as strangers in a strange place.

From the school they were marched in crocodile fashion to their billets. The local inhabitants must have found it equally strange to have little London kids billeted on them, a lot of them Jewish, bringing with them a strange culture and equally strange ideas.

The Jewish influx to the royal borough did not make a great impact on the indigenous residents. I can't remember any Hassidic Jews with long coats and sideburns wandering the ancient streets. At that time Windsor was a fairly quiet royal town, not geared to hoards of tourists as it is today.

The castle rose majestic at the top of the hill and the streets fell away reducing in size and wealth as they went. There was a fairly large proportion of fine Victorian and Edwardian villas that had enough rooms for the evacuees. Into these houses the Jewish people moved with their small belongings and hopes fastened in their suitcases. The children were mostly billetted in other accommodation, away from their parents.

My parents were already there as my father had found himself a not-so-royal barber job, a couple of years earlier. They lived by the river in a sweet 1930's terrace house, Their days were spent in a hazy pink glow expecting life to drift on in a roses-round-the-door manner ever after, amen. Life has a way of mucking up one's expectations in a big way.

To help pay the rent Mrs Turner had moved into the front room to live, as she thought, as a 'distressed gentlefolk' in quiet seclusion. What eventually she was plunged into was very distressing and certainly far from gentle.

Then came the war, then came the relations and then came my GRANDMOTHER. Whether the war or my grandmother caused the biggest bang in my parents life I cannot say, but for my poor mother neither event was welcome.

When the bombs first dropped on London the relations, en masse, swooped on the love nest in Windsor like a hundred cuckoos. My father had joined the army and my mother had fled to work in a John Lewis shop, Caleys, opposite the castle. The money came in handy but the respite from the relatives was the main reason for the daily departure to work.

The relatives or 'aunts' had a pecking order in the house with my grandmother, as eldest sister, ruling the roost. My mother, a quiet soul, drifted about just dreaming about the time when this nightmare would be over and her Lochinvar

17

would come riding in out of the west, or in this case, east, to carry her away on the back of his white charger.

If my mother saw life through a hazy glow Mrs Turner saw it through an alcoholic mist and I only think she survived the relatives by viewing them through the bottom of a glass.

The aunts were either sisters or sisters-in-law of my grandmother so they were actually great aunts to me. Looking back I wonder where they all slept and I have been told that three of them slept under a table in the back room. This was only a small terraced house and through my childish eyes they all looked huge so I can only assume the house acted like a terraced Tardis.

I do remember one particular aunt sitting up in bed peeling potatoes which didn't strike me as particularly strange at the time. Not like the home of our dear Queen just up the road!

The kitchen was another dimension of the war. Two women in a kitchen is an explosion so with about six of them all fighting for the stove, the sink and any available working space, it was more like the prelude to Hiroshima. There was always the complication of keeping the kitchen kosher with Mrs Turner stewing rabbit (definitely not kosher) on one of the rings and my grandmother brewing the endless chicken soup.

The smells that emanated from the kitchen were a mixture of fried fish, boiling chicken, stewing rabbit and dirty washing-up water. This was ethnic mixing par excellence. I remember one piece of very wet cod flying across the kitchen from my grandmother's hands in the direction of a screaming red-faced aunt. The projectile landed slap bang on her nose, the target for which it was intended!

I, of course, loved it all. Standing by the kitchen door I would watch the antics of the adults and thought it was all great fun. War-time rations didn't help, but nobody seemed to be hungry. A modern social worker viewing the scene would have thought the atmosphere totally wrong for a young child, but to me it home and altogether wonderful.

If it became too raucous I would retreat to Mrs Turner's room and watch her steadily drink her way through the rich ruby while she mended her 'combs'. The 'combs' were three pairs of combinations, the all-in-one garment with a trapdoor in the bottom for the human functions. They were originally made of very fine wool, but by the time my eyes feasted upon them they were kept together by finely-darned patches.

Mrs Turner wore these combinations every day of her life and was often seen in the front garden, adorned only in her combs, drunk, looking for something she had lost. Somebody from the house would drag her inside, and she was never less than polite. She would sit for hours, drunk or sober, mending her treasures and dreaming of better days. To facilitate the darning Mrs Turner had a wooden darning mushroom over which the latest hole would be stretched. Sometimes when she was drunk or drunkish, she would miss the hole and just darn a good piece. One of her little sayings while darning ran as follows:

"Stitch, stitch, stitch, in poverty, hunger and dirt, till over the stitches she fell asleep and sewed them all in a dream."

I never saw her take off the said combs but I suppose she must have done when she had a wash "as far as possible". I don't think she ever ventured into the bathroom upstairs. Her washing was done in a cracked metal bowl on a wooden chair in front of the fire.

One of the other great pleasures of my life with Mrs Turner was playing cards. She taught me how to play rummy and cribbage and I was always in charge of the matchsticks to place in the holes of the cribbage board.

Mrs Turner played a lot of patience and I learnt from her the many different ways of playing the game. I was never allowed to cheat!

I learnt so much from that glorious lady who had come down in the world having divorced her no-good husband. She would often say to herself in her cups, "To think I have come to this, living in one room with all I own in a couple of suitcases".

She did have a son, Reg, who was in the Merchant Navy doing the Atlantic Run. Reg, who had been suckled on rich ruby, came home on leave very rarely but when he did they had great celebrations. As Lady Diana Spencer once said, "There were three of us in that marriage", and with Mrs Turner and Reg there were three of them in that relationship, she, him and rich ruby.

I lived my young life as it were moving through an imaginary revolving door. The door went 360 degrees from the explosive, warm and funny world of the Jews through to the genteel, but drunk, world of a Christian lady. When I had had enough of one world I sallied through the revolving door to the other.

Over all these diverse characters was my dearly beloved grandmother. All 5′ 2″ of her she reigned supreme in my life and although she has been dead for 35 years she is never far from my shoulder.

THE SYNAGOGUE PLUS JESUS

A Jewish community needs a rabbi and with the rabbi, the synagogue. Windsor during the war had both. Rabbi Jacobovitz, father of the former British Chief Rabbi Jacobovitz, had fled from Germany and found himself and his children in Windsor. The family, of which there were several boys and one girl, lived in a flat in a small street behind the main shopping thoroughfare, Peascod Street.

Mrs Jacobovitz was a beautiful person and was greatly loved by the community as was her husband. It was no surprise to me that one of the sons became such a well-loved Chief Rabbi, respected by the great and the good and having a knighthood bestowed upon him.

He was a great favourite of Mrs Thatcher and she looked to him for spiritual and moral guidance when the Church of England was trying to placate all and leading none. The country as a whole mourned when he died in 1999.

The synagogue was a makeshift affair above a non-denominational church near the castle. Early on Friday nights and Saturday mornings the warden of the synagogue would perambulate around the hall turning the pictures of Jesus to the wall! At the end of the service Jesus was reinstated for the admiration of his Christian community.

21

The church above which was the synagogue.

As a child I was fascinated by the men in their prayer shawls shaking and mumbling their prayers. As Jewish belief is that each man has a direct line to God, everyone can say their prayers at their own speed. Consequently some prayers were finished before others and the general sound was of chaos. The problem was that once a man had finished his prayer he would start to chat to the next 'finished' prayer so although the praying would end the noise wouldn't.

They had much to pray about at this time as they knew that if Hitler successfully invaded Great Britain they would be the first to suffer. They were mostly the old and the very young as the other men were already in the forces.

Some had escaped from Europe and knew first-hand what Hitler would do to them had they come under his rule. Of the concentration camps there were only whispers.

On my father's pay book which I discovered years later, where the world 'religion' was printed, my father had written

2

(I) SOLDIER'S NAME and DESCRIPTION on ATTESTATION.

Army Number _1083346_

Surname (in capitals) _MICHAELSON_

Christian Names (in full) _~~DECEASED~~_

Date of Birth _3/5/11._

Place of Birth.
- Parish ....
- In or near the town of ....
- In the county of ....

Trade on Enlistment _Raincoat Manufacturer_ ....

Nationality of Father at birth ....

Nationality of Mother at birth ....

Religious Denomination ███████ _AGNOSTIC_

Approved Society ....

Membership No. ....

Enlisted at _Maidstone_ On _10-40_

For the :— _Army Class_ _DECEASED_

* Regular Army.   * Supplementary Reserve
* Territorial Army.   * Army Reserve Section B.
        * Strike out those inapplicable.

For ....years with the Colours and............years in the Reserve.

Signature of Soldier ....

Date _22/2/44_

My father's Pay Book with the religious denomination, Jewish, cut out and replaced by Agnostic, presumably in case he was captured by the Germans.

'Agnostic'. Whether this was true or whether it was a cover if he was ever captured, I do not know – probably a bit of both. These are the sorts of details about my parents of which I know nothing.

I found the whole of the services fascinating even if I didn't understand what was going on. It was the theatre of it all, the music, the prayer shawls and above all the Torah scrolls. On a Sabbath morning the scrolls would be taken out of the makeshift ark, the outer vestments were disrobed and two strong arms would lift the sacred scrolls high in the air so that the community could see them.

I believe this is a very ancient tradition dating back to Biblical times when all writing was done on scrolls so in this way the congregation could see from where the readings were being gleaned. The scrolls are made up of the five books of Moses, the first five books of the Old Testament.

The scrolls are hand-written by a scribe and have to be absolutely perfect. If the writer makes one mistake, even the last word, the whole thing has to be done again! Will they ever be done on computers, I ask myself. I think not somehow.

The Torah is written on parchment made by a specified section of the hide of a kosher animal (though not necessarily slaughtered according to Jewish ritual). The method of cleaning and softening of the hide has changed throughout the centuries.

During talmudic times, salt and barley flour were sprinkled on the skins, which were then soaked in the juice of gallnuts. There is, however, a reference to the use of dog's dung for this purpose, a rite no longer in use thank goodness. These days the skins are softened by soaking them in clear water for two days, after which the hair is removed by soaking the hides in limewater for nine days. Finally, the skins are rinsed and dried and the creases ironed out with presses.

When reading from the scrolls a pointer is used so that the sweat of the hand does not marr the letters. These pointers are usually made of silver and are in the shape of a hand with a pointed finger.

In the early years of Judaism it was the custom to use gold lettering. According to the letter of Aristeas, the Torah presented by Eleazer the high priest to Ptolemy Philadelphus was written in gold letters. However, such ostentation was later forbidden. Synagogues are organised by a committee who have a great deal of power as they can hire or fire the rabbi, set the synagogue fees and run the day-to-day management. The chairman during most part of the war was Mr Lewis Gould.

Mr and Mrs Gould had two daughter, Isabel and Rosita, the latter being my first head girl at Windsor Grammar School. We lost touch with each other for many years, but met again and remain firm friends.

The women sat at the back of the synagogue usually chatting and catching up with the gossip. A few prayed but not many of the women bothered to praise their God when Mrs Cohen's errant daughter was of far more interest. Women ruled the roost and the men thought they ruled the synagogue.

In retrospect my feelings are that the women based their relationship with God in line with their relationship with their families. God would be quite happy with them if their kitchens were kosher and their chopped liver perfection. The rest the men could get sorted out. As this attitude has lasted thousands of years who is to say they were wrong.

As Judaism is a way of life and food is the sustenance of life, maybe these yiddishe mamas had found the meaning of life that the theologians and philosophers had missed. Perhaps those with their noses in the cooking pot rather than in the great tomes had really found the answer. Who needs a book when you are hungry?

I remember Chief Rabbi Jacobovitz as a very devout young man. He never took his eyes off his book unless it was to close them in communion with his God. With his mother looking after his bodily needs he had the luxury of feeding his soul.

His father was a very warm and lovable character. When my parents died he put me on his knee and though I can't remember what he said I can still bring to mind the feel of his arms around me, embracing me with love.

All the festivals were held in the synagogue. I was always a very shy child and I hated having to join in with the other children taking part in the festivities.

On one memorable occasion there was a festival where all the children marched around the hall carrying a lit candle stuck into an apple. My candle, of course, progressed in a forward slope away from its anchorage and began to set alight the hair of the girl in front of me. The hair began to sizzle and so did her mother and I was yanked out of the proceedings in great disgrace.

Festivals came and went with their various traditions, but the High Holidays, Rosh Hashonna (New Year) and Yom Kippur (Day of Atonement) were the times when the synagogue was full to bursting. Anybody who called themselves Jewish went to the Synagogue. The congregation all had their various reasons for going, not least that they could not be seen not to be going.

The High Holidays were the times for the ladies to dress up and be admired. Perhaps they thought God would favour them if they wore their best outfits. As this was war time and clothing coupons at a premium, most of the clothes were *a la mode* in the thirties.

I would turn around in the seat and gaze for many an hour into the dead faces of the fox furs draped around sloping shoulders. The little brown eyes of the long-dead fox would peer at me as if resentful of the fact that he had to spent the rest of his eternity wrapped round the body of some overweight matron. The legs would dangle and the magnificent brush was a symbol of wealth. Most of the foxes looked slightly moth-eaten and are now seen popping up at the back of attics tucked away from the horrified eyes of the animal rights campaigners.

Fashion in the thirties relied on other animals. The matching crocodile shoes and handbag were things which came with marrying 'money'. Not many of Windsor congregations rose to those heady heights though ordinary handbags there were a-plenty.

Out of these handbags came an assortment of goodies and on Yom Kippur snuggling in with the Max Factor loose powder compact and lipstick was the smelling salts. These little bottles were filled with salvolatile, ammonium carbonate, known as smelling salts.

As Yom Kippur was a 24-hour fast sniffing at the salts was to prevent you from falling horizontally on to the floor through hunger. The genteel way of doing this was to lift the spotted veil of your hat and sniff quietly from the bottle. As most of the ladies were as genteel as a cart horse the sniffing sounded rather like the noise emanating from beneath a towel when sniffing Vick.

On one occasion I managed to get hold of a bottle and sniffed as if I was taking my last breath. It practically was, as my head went several feet upwards and my eyes watered like Niagra. Glue sniffers of today are mere amateurs compared with the synagogue ladies when in full sniffing flight.

Yom Kippur is the Day of Repentance and the holiest day in the Jewish calendar. I don't know what sins these frightened Jews were repenting, but as an adult I have felt that perhaps

God should ask repentance of his people for what he has allowed to happen in the world. "Them's fighting words", but ones which must have been thought by every thinking person over the centuries.

The synagogue was a cacophony of sound ranging from the Cantor's singing, the prayers praying and the ladies sniffing and talking. In the midst of this wonderful noise came the blasting of the shofar, the ritual ram's horn.

Certainly one of the strangest pieces of ritual paraphernalia is the shofar. The smooth, curved ram's horn has an aura of the primitive and seems a throwback to hoary antiquity. The horn is blown at various times during the service and it has a sound that seems to penetrate to the depths of your soul. Such is the power of the shofar that one could well imagine that the end of the world will be preluded by its sound.

The mediaeval rabbi, Maimonides, said there was message implicit within the practice.

"Sleepers, awake from your sleep! Slumberers arouse yourselves from your slumber! Search your deeds and return to your repentance and remember your Creator."

The people in that tiny make-shift synagogue prayed to their God to save them from the war and mainly to save them from Hitler. To me the shofar has never had more meaning.

Leading up to the synagogue was an iron staircase and most of the children spent their time playing games up and down the steps and generally making a racket. Every so often the warden would come out and remonstrate and for five minutes we settled down to laugh in whispers about the various occupants of the synagogue.

The dusty prayer hall was nearly always full. There is nothing like a war to concentrate the mind on the Almighty and get whatever help you could pray him into giving. Knowing what Hitler would do to the community had he actually invaded guaranteed a large attendance and the synagogue was very much part of my early life.

Naturally I had not the slightest idea of what the war was really about but whenever I asked for anything the reply was, "No, don't you know there is a war on". The news was also a major part of life and I would wonder what would be on the news, or if, indeed there would be news when the war was over.

The synagogue, like all such institutions, had a a Ladies Guild. I suppose it was like a Jewish version of the Women's Institute without the jam and definitely without the decorum. Jerusalem hardly got much of an input either compared with who made the best biscuits and who hadn't paid their membership fees.

The ladies busied themselves making the food for the festivals and even with the rationing they managed to make the traditional foods for each occasion.

My grandmother was the treasurer of the Ladies Guild and we would spend hours calling at various houses trying to collect the fees. Most of the ladies were always OUT.

Windsor, the most English and royal town in the country, had beneath its ramparts a replica of the East European shtetl. Most people will recognise the shtetl from 'Fiddler on the Roof' where the Jewish community live alongside their indigenous neighbours until some calamity makes them move.

This Windsor shtetl came and went within about ten years at the most. I feel that if Hitler had known it was there Windsor Castle would have been a target of lots more bombs.

"BOBA"

"I remember everyone, but most of all I remember Mama". That was the opening line of an old black and white film. In my case it was "I remember everyone but most of all I remember Boba". This is the yiddish name for grandmother and for the whole of her life this is what I called her. She called me "My Clare", never the noun without the possessive article.

When my mother died she took me over which, at 60 years old, was no mean feat. I don't think she thought for a moment that she wouldn't and as far as she was concerned 60 was no age at all.

Boba had already taken over the house long before my mother died as the latter couldn't cope with the relatives and only lived for letters from my father. At this time during the war everyone had their own tragedies and one little six-year-old orphan was no big deal.

At this time I was sleeping on the two chairs in Mrs Turner's room and the relatives slept wherever they lay their bodies which was sometimes under the dining room table. Where Boba slept at this time I have no idea, but as she was not high on 'niceties' it would have been wherever her body laid itself down.

Somehow I have to describe her, but one can mainly only

Boba reading the News Chronicle by the Sabbath candles.

give a picture of the outside layer, her true beauty lay inside. Physically she was about 5ft.1in. with salt & pepper hair screwed back into a bun. Her body which must have been an ample 12st. (who knew about such things as dieting, particularly in the war) was covered in several layers. One of the layers was a huge pink corset with strings. Underneath the corset was tucked a red thermogen wool pad to prevent lumbago. Every night when she divested herself of these tight, itchy garments she would rotate her vest on her skin to eliminate the itching. "Ahh, that's better", she would breathe as she relieved herself of the torment of the wrappings.

From this you may gather that fashion was not quite her thing and in the winter if she couldn't find her gloves, a pair of old socks would do. On her feet she flopped along in flat black shoes, but on special occasions such as weddings and barmitzvahs she would don shiny black shoes with heels.

I always felt slightly ashamed of her in her heels as it wasn't quite right for an old, old lady to be wearing such flighty things. There is nothing more embarrassing than a little girl whose grandmother wore high heels and spoke loud yiddish.

The stockings were not quite Nora Batty, but sometimes the suspenders which hung flaccid from the pink corset parted company from the stockings and then Boba would stop in her tracks, hoist up the skirt and hook the leggings back in place. Another moment of total embarrassment.

Inside this dishevelled shell lay a mind sharp as a needle and a heart as soft as butter. She loved me completely without reservation and mostly she loved the rest of the world, but not always. Some people she hated, but the dichotomy was that although she disliked them intensely she would give them her last penny.

When Mrs. Next-door with whom there was an on-going battle about chickens and practically everything else, was dumped into the street by her daughter, my grandmother took her in and looked after her for five years. This was after the time-period of this book which ends in 1950. The other neighbours put forth not a hand of friendship.

This was no genteel, little old lady passing by, this was a hurricane of love, hate, wit, wisdom, charisma and courage. I will never be half the person she was, and in my heart, still is.

Rachel Feldman was born in Poland in the year 1884. Her father, a tailor, had married the eldest daughter of a family in the village. He was actually in love with the second daughter, but the rule and commandment was that the second daughter could not marry before her eldest sister.

So to be able to remain near the woman he loved he

married her sister and had two children with her – a boy and a girl. Either fate or God was on his side as the wife died and he was then able to marry the woman he wanted.

With anti-semitism on the high in Russia and Poland, Soloman and Hudis plus the two children boarded the boat for England. They landed with hundreds of others at London Docks and were given the name Solomons by the customs officer who couldn't spell Schloshkslovitch.

They settled in the east end of London where relatives and friends, old hands at immigration, helped them start a new life away from the constant fear in Poland. Probably with the upheaval and strangeness of starting life anew, Hudis had two miscarriages, but the third pregnancy produced Rachel, a much wanted and much-loved child.

The pair got on with their lives and ten more much-loved children arrived. Rachel being the second eldest, next to sister, Leah, had a loving but hard childhood. When she got home tired from school, piles of dishes waited for her in the kitchen sink. There was no hot water and no heating in the back kitchen so she washed the dishes in the icy cold water and stood on the cold floorboards to do it.

She would stand at the kitchen window drowned in dishes while the street children outside played with hoops and danced a jig in time to the barrel-organ man's music. These frivolities were not for her and she vowed her children would never work in her kitchen. They never did.

On the floorboards was straw that her father carried home once a month from the market. With the straw came the fleas and her chapped legs were emblazoned with flea bites. Every family in those sordid East End back streets had the same lives so nobody thought they were worse off than anybody else.

On her thirteenth birthday she left school, no waiting for the end of term in those days. On your birthday you were out and into the world of work. In Rachel's case it was her father's workshop at the top of the house.

In the workshop were about a dozen people, sewing machinists, felling hands, buttonhole makers and pressers making cheap garments for about half a crown an item. In today's world the workshop would be closed down immediately as both a health and fire hazard. In those days it was a way of making a living, a poor but just about adequate living. Who thought about health hazards, the whole of life was a health hazard.

Into this sweat shop, owned by her father, 13-year-old Rachel learnt how to fell (tack) jackets, trousers, waistcoats and overcoats of very rough material. Once proficient at that she moved onto buttonholes a really skilled trade which earned a few more pennies a week.

The employees, mostly Solomon's children, worked from eight in the morning until eight at night. Thank goodness for Sabbath, for that meant stopping at nightfall on Friday evening until Sunday morning. Sometimes they worked on Saturday evening if there was a rush of work.

When Moses brought down the tablets of stone with the commandment of having the Sabbath off, what a brilliant piece of legislation for Jewish workers worldwide. One wonders if God started his incarnation in a Jewish tailoring workshop!

Although Hudis was a very religious woman she was liberal with her beloved family. After the Friday night dinner round the candlelit table they were able to go out and enjoy themselves. This was unusual in an orthodox Jewish household but Hudis knew if you kept your children on too tight a rein they would break it.

My grandmother loved to dance and she went with her eldest stepbrother, Wolfie, to the many dances held in the east end at the turn of the century. I gather she was a wow at the Veleta!

Sixty years later we would sit round the dying embers of the coal fire after the lodgers had departed for bed, and she would regale me stories of 'the bad old days' as she called them. She didn't remember her youth with a pink glow but as days of poverty, cold and hard work.

However corny it may sound there was lots of love and lots of fun in the workshop. Innocent games played by very innocent people. There was no need for enforced 'pc' as it was already in existence with the Jewish way of life.

Rachel had great sympathy for the suffragette movement and the burgeoning Labour Party and would attend meetings of both organisations as often as she could. She remained a staunch member of the Labour Party until the Suez crisis when she and Hugh Gaitskell parted company. I don't think he noticed!

One of my abiding memories of her was reading the News Chronicle late at night and discarding each page round her feet as she read it. She would slip out of the pile like walking out of knickers and leave yesterday's news to light the fire in the morning.

Rachel being an intelligent and fast worker was eventually made foreman of the workshop, much to the chagrin of the men. This was 1905 and women did not normally give men orders, and particularly not a slip of a girl like her. She gave one man the sack for being very rude to her and proceeded to advertise for another worker. In walked my grandfather.

He was a young, very handsome immigrant from Riga in Latvia, with empty pockets and a good education. His education would not get him a good job in England at the time as immigrants were limited to two or three trades such as tailoring, peddling and cabinet making. The working laws for immigrants would be changed many years later.

They were married in 1909 and the next day he was back at work and she was a bride in a suite of 2 rooms upstairs in a tiny house round the corner from her mother. Three children followed, my two uncles, Alf and Sydney, and my mother, Nettie. I don't think her gift was for choosing names!

Determined not to have a gaggle of children like her mother, she visited Marie Stopes clinic in Holloway, London, in 1921 This was considered to be a terrible thing in the Jewish community, but this didn't bother her. She had seen too much poverty in her childhood to perpetuate the system.

My grandfather eventually gave up tailoring and the couple tried several unsuccessful enterprises, one of them making sweets. Eventually they opened a stall in Berwick Street market in the West End of London, selling stockings. My grandmother stood in the gutter of this street for 26 years and finally went bankrupt.

One of my prize possessions is her visiting card which reads: 'Madam Feldman, Hosiery specialist, outside 26 Berwick Street." She had a maid at home looking after the children and every afternoon the said maid would come out to the market in her black dress and starched pinny and serve my grandmother tea on a tray! Standards were not to be dropped even in the gutter.

These were very hard years, out in all weathers and working long hours. On top of this there were two other hosiery stalls in the market – either side of her. Each customer was fought over by the three stallholders all trying to make a week's profit from the small pickings.

Once one of the other stallholders set fire to my grandmother's stall hoping to eliminate the opposition. There were no niceties in market business in those days. Boba managed fortunately to put out the fire before too much damage was done to the stock. I think some of the stockings had a smoky haze about them!

Many of my grandmother's best customers were the show girls from the nearby theatres and the prostitutes from the surrounding streets.

For my grandfather who was from genteel stock, the life was nearly intolerable and he smoked Turkish cigarettes until they killed him with TB. My grandmother was a widow at 40 with three children to keep, and a failing business. Most of the profits went on doctors fees trying to cure the TB.

My grandfather eventually died of consumption and with no other door open to her, Boba rolled up her sleeves, put a smile on her face and continued in the gutter until the war. She never re-married.

When the 'phoney' war came to an end she moved down to Brighton to get away from Hitler's bombs. For several months by the sea she led a gipsy life, moving from one set of lodgings to another, not getting an income from anywhere.

She managed, after a long struggle, to pay off her creditors and life began to look up. Then Hitler marched into Poland. Her eldest son, Alf, had married, my mother was married and living in Windsor and the second son, Syd, was due to go off to the Army.

Syd had gone off with her to Brighton until the call-up papers caught up with him. At this point Boba realised that Windsor was her only option and left Brighton Pavilion for Windsor Castle. Nothing less than royal connections for her!

Into the pink glow of my mother's life trundled my grandmother with an assortment of bags. The pink glow was evaporating quickly as my father had gone off to serve King and Country in the Royal Artillery. My grandmother arrived plus the assorted relatives and Windsor became the Promised Land.

This chapter is devoted to a description of Boba, but as an addendum I should add that I was born in 1939 and during these war years I was very very quiet, shy and vastly inquisitive, breathing in the world around me and hugging it to myself.

THE FAMILY PLUS ONE

To me my mother is a set of polyphoto pictures. A dozen inch by inch photographs on a sheet. Not much of a memory, more of an icon. These photographs were all the rage in the forties and everyone was having them done. I presume the photographer had come to the shop where she worked as secretary to the general manager, and did a set of pictures for her. She probably had them taken for my father because several of the pictures are missing.

The shop was Caleys of Windsor, a very posh department store where the Queen shopped and the aristocratic ladies of the area all had credit. You had to be rich not to pay at the time of purchase!

Caleys is part of the John Lewis Partnership and still flourishes opposite the castle. I worked there for six months on their house magazine, but I was too much of a rebel to last in that cut-glass atmosphere.

For someone who can remember so much about childhood, I have only one memory of my mother washing my face in the bathroom. Beyond that there is nothing except a wedding picture and these polyphotographs that my grandmother had stuck at the back of a drawer.

For some reason of her own. after my mother died Boba

Polyphotos of my mother two years before she died.

never mentioned her. She did not and had not existed as far the household were concerned. It was one of those subjects that were never mentioned, like sex and Jesus Christ.

At some time or another Boba must have said to everybody that her daughter must not be mentioned in front of the child. This rule was kept and neither of my parents, after their deaths, ever existed in that house.

It had been, after all, their home and they were gone like a puff of wind. Not even the name remained on the rent book. Somebody somewhere must have erased their names and substituted my grandmother's. I suppose that summed up the situation completely.

Maybe Boba thought it would upset me to have them spoken about. I just don't know, and the subject remained a taboo until she died aged 79, when I was 25. Never once did she or I mention their names.

We spent many, many hours talking together over the years, but my parents' names never came up. Nettie and Bernard were ghosts of a tragic past and left to fade away into oblivion. To this day I know very little about my mother. All I get from the few remaining members of the family that knew her is that she was quiet, clever and very much a lady.

That anyone in my raucous family was a lady is an astonishment in itself. How she managed that accolade is a mystery and I can only guess that she took after my grandfather who was, according to the same sources, a gentleman.

Nettie was the youngest child, with two older brothers, Alf and Sidney. She was the brightest of the three and went to to Buckingham Gate Central School which was under the auspices of the London County Council. I know she went there because I have a copy of David Copperfield which she won at the school. This was the Matthew Arnold Prize. What she had done to win this book I have no idea, but I guess it was some sort of English prize.

Beyond this there is a black hole until she met my father. He had come down from Manchester to seek his fortune in the bright lights. He lived as a lodger in Boba's house in London.

Apparently after coming out at Oxford Street Station he had walked along Berwick Street market and happened to ask my Uncle Alf standing at the stall, if he knew of any digs in the area. He introduced this stranger to my grandmother and the young man had immediately found a home.

There my parents met, fell in love, married and moved down to Windsor for work. There had been an advertisement in the paper for a barber in the royal borough, Father applied and the rest, as they say, is history, if only a short one.

Theirs will remain a love story unsullied by the vicissitudes of a long marriage. They were married in London in 1938 and at the end of 1939 he had gone off to war with the Royal Artillery, leaving her to cope with me and the family. She didn't do this very well.

According to his last remaining sister, my father was an outgoing chap, full of fun and life. But the fun and the life were lost at the battle of Monte Casino. He was a gunner but it did not stop him being a target for a German shell.

I was born at the beginning of 1939 and by August 1944 my father was dead, leaving my distracted mother to last just four months. Apparently I have gleaned that somebody said, when she was in the depths of despair, "What about Clare?" to which she replied, "Clare will be all right". How she justified herself that I would be "all right" I have no idea, but I suppose in the end she was correct.

I believe that she lived just for love of this one man and when he was gone there was nothing else left. Her cupboard was bare. She was too quiet and too gentle to cope with a

My father's grave in Florence, Italy.

My father taken in Tel Aviv whilst on leave from the regiment.

EFWG 8

Address any reply to:-
The Under-Secretary of
State, and quote:-

THE WAR OFFICE,
EFFECTS BRANCH,
EDGE LANE,
LIVERPOOL, 7.

D/ *151369.* (Effects)
609.6.

24 MAY 1946   194

Sir/Madam,

I am directed to inform you that the sum of £ **23 : — : —** d.
is due from Army Funds to the late

Gnr. B. B. Michaelson

in respect of:-

	£	s	d
War Gratuity	23	0	0

No Will executed by the *deceased* having
been brought to the notice of this Department, a draft for

£ **23 : — : —** d. in your favour as his *Mother of late widow of the
late soldier* is enclosed, *in part reimbursement for funeral Expn
of the late Mrs. Michaelson* I am, Sir/Madam,
Your obedient Servant,

Mrs. R. Feldman.

*Letter from the War Office dated May 1946 to my grandmother, informing
her that as mother of the deceased, Nettie Michaelson (my mother), she
should receive £23 as part reimbursement for the above's funeral expenses.*

home bursting at the seams. Her sanctuary had gone amidst the hurly-burly of the house and there was literally no resting place.

I don't even know and cannot work out, where she slept. Every inch was taken up by somebody's sleeping arrangements. She is buried next to my grandmother in the Jewish cemetary at Edmonton, North London. He is in the British War Cemetary, in Florence. One hopes that there is an after-life so that they are at one because they didn't even have the luck to be buried together.

I have been to the Florence cemetary and seen the grave, but what does a name on a tombstone mean if you have no memories of the person behind the name. I do have a certificate from the Internet saying where and when my father died, but it sits in a frame on a table and gets dusted occasionally. He went to war with a life in front of him and ended up in a frame.

His name also appears on a glass panel in Windsor Parish Church amongst the other heroes of the town who never came back. For a man brought up in a very religious Jewish home in Manchester it is strange that he is remembered in a parish church in Windsor. *C'est la vie!*

The aunts were made of tougher stuff and thankfully survived the war. They were, in fact, my great aunts as they were of Boba's generation.

Aunt Dora was Boba's youngest sister, the last of a line of eleven children. She was married to a Jewish chap revelling in the name of Jock. How he came by this Scottish appellation is lost in the mists of time, but Jock it was.

They had two children, Ronald and Helen, both of whom were billeted in Windsor. Aunt Dora's claim to fame was that she was a pianist in the silent movies and right up to her 95th birthday she could play the piano. Her short-term memory eventually went but not the old tunes played over a long lifetime.

Aunt Hannah who was married to Harry (of whom later), was the 'clever' one of the family. She had come from Russia as a qualified dispensing chemist which was very advanced for a woman in those days. She was small of stature but large of brain and was respected by everyone.

Her daughter, Betty, a schoolgirl at that time, was with her parents in the house and I have strong memories of her repeating her French verbs whilst asleep. Betty had been billeted elsewhere but preferred to be with her parents. This book is dedicated to her as I know how fond her memories are of Windsor.

The third Aunt was Annie, married to Boba's youngest brother, David. Annie was a sweet soul, Jewish mother material who just lived for her Dave and two children, Martin and Cyril. Martin was evacuated at another house in Windsor and Cyril was in the house. Annie had been a cigarette maker in her youth, a Jewish Carmen if you like. However, I don't think Bizet would have conjured her up for the role!

David was an ambulance driver in London for the whole period of the war, one of the many brave souls left in the capital.

Filling the last bit of available space was Aunt Esther, married to uncle Issy, yet another of Boba's brothers. Esther was the beam of sunshine in the house. You never saw her without a smile and she and my grandmother would laugh like drains at almost everything. Esther had come to Windsor because her daughter, Sheila, had been evacuated there with her school.

With Boba, myself, Mrs Turner and various other people coming and going, this was the complement of the house. I understand that three people slept under the living room table.

Perhaps this explains why my relationship with my mother was minimal. There were too many other 'mothers' and in my small mind one was as good as the other for a cuddle.

There was no shortage of love for me in that house and of insecurity I knew nothing. I was like Puck girdling the house every forty minutes, listening to all the laughter, anger, frustration and love that reverberated around me.

Yiddish was the language of the home except for Mrs Turner's room where the English of Celia Johnson was spoken albeit slightly slurred! I had no toys but the house was my toy box and all my dolls were alive and such fun to play with.

Although not a blood relative or even Jewish, I must honour our next door neighbour, Mrs. Ethel King. This wonderful country woman was another mother to me and the other side of my grandmother's coin. She and Boba complemented each other in practically every way.

Boba would do all Mrs King's writing jobs and Mrs. King did all Boba's sewing, knitting, chicken information and other practical jobs. Mrs King was the hub around which the street revolved. If anybody wanted anything or needed anything it was to Mrs. King they turned.

She brought up two daughters of her own, Nancy and Muriel, and adopted and fostered many others. Mrs. King was always there to lay out a body or comfort the bereaved. Her eldest daughter, Nancy, was a hairdresser and there were great plans for after the war when she and my father would open a hairdressing salon together. Another lost dream.

She and Boba communed over the garden fence. Why this was I don't know, but all business was done out the back. Mrs. King also had chickens, but somehow hers were contained in a clean run and never made messes in the garden. "Next door's garden is always greener", and in my case, clear of chicken mess!

Mrs King although in her forties, didn't have any teeth. At least she had a set of false ones which she kept well hidden. She could eat anything with her gums and everyone loved her with or without dentures. One day she put the false teeth in to take me up to the castle to watch the Garter procession and I asked her to take them out as it just wasn't her. She happily agreed. I never see the Queen in her Garter robes without thinking of Mrs. King's teeth!

There was nothing practical that Mrs King couldn't do and she was our regular chimney sweep. I loved it when it was time to have the chimney swept as I was given a very important job. It was my huge responsibility to stand in the garden and watch for the brush to come whooshing through the chimney stack. When the brush had found the daylight it meant that the whole of the chimney had been cleaned. At this point I had to shout out that the brush had come out and Mrs. King could then retrieve the long sticks.

The excitement I felt waiting for the brush to appear knew no bounds. Perhaps it was equivalent of waiting for Father Christmas to come 'down' the chimney, but in this case it was for the brush to come 'up' the chimney. Nobody has ever seen the old man in red but I had seen the brush emerging out of the darkness and swaying in the daylight.

About this time I had read a poem by William Blake called *The Chimney Sweep* and I loved it because it could have been me. It ran:

> When my mother died I was very young
> And my father sold me while yet my tongue
> Could scarcely cry: "'Weep! 'weep! 'weep! 'weep!"
> So your chimneys I sweep, and in soot I sleep.

There were six very sad verses to this poem and I read it so

Mrs Ethel King, our next-door neighbour.

often I knew it by heart.

It was a day of great importance when Mrs King cleaned the chimney as everything had to be covered up to protect it from the soot. Somehow this system never worked because by the time the brushes came out of the chimney, the room, Boba, Mrs King, I and all the furniture were covered in the 'black stuff'.

The next couple of days were spent frantically cleaning up though, in fact, it was probably just moving the soot and dust from one place to another. Can you imagine cleaning up this terrible mess with only a handbroom with which to do it. The whole house joined in mainly getting in each others way.

Now came the big moment for Boba to decide that the room needed decorating as the soot had 'lingered'. In came Mrs King again, this time with different brushes.

Decorating meant the back room as it was considered impossible to do Mrs Turner's room as she was never upright long enough to be of any help! As a lot of people slept in the back room everything had to be done in a day.

Mrs King spent the hours painting over the soot on the ceiling and covering over the filthy walls with terrible wallpaper. Boba's choice of wallpaper would not have featured on the cover of *Homes and Gardens*. "At least its clean", was what she uttered standing in the newly decorated horror. The aunts couldn't have cared less as long as they could get to bed.

Boba and Mrs king would regularly go to Slough cattle market to buy chickens to supplement the ones that had landed on the dining table. I usually went with them where the delirium of bidding for the chickens against somebody else was immense. It was all such fun even if I hated the birds once they came home.

On one occasion Mrs King decided she would like a goose

instead of the chickens. This bird, however, was not a great success as he frightened everyone to death when they tried to enter Mrs. King's garden. He soon landed up on the dining table, but how he was ever caught let alone strangled I never found out.

Mrs King knew nothing about anti-semitism and accepted the queer folk next door as nothing strange. She survived my grand-mother many years and I loved her deeply.

How two such wonderful women of a great cultural divide came together is nothing short of miraculous. Each respected the other's way of life and both held out their hands to each other whenever they were needed. If only the world could revolve on their example.

THE COMMUNAL

Apart from the makeshift synagogue the Jewish community needed a meeting place for social functions and food. This need was satisfied by a long wooden, single storey building attached to the Thames Hotel opposite the river.

This building is now a tourist-type pub where visitors drink their welcome 'pint' unaware of the building's previous use. Should they know I doubt if they would care much that a lot of war-time Jewish refugees from London played out their hopes in this hall.

In those days the hall was long, dusty and drab. Round the walls were an assortment of uncut-moquet armchairs, mainly red which, in their lifetime, had never been cleaned. Nobody seemed to be in charge of cleaning the windows either so they matched the grime of the furniture. What point in cleaning windows when at any moment a bomb could blast them to smithereens.

Through the windows a few rays of sunshine would penetrate and in the rays the dust would show up like a solid strip of moving particles. Anyone with chest complaints did not fare well in the 'communal'.

The floor was just plain boards and scattered around were odd trestle tables. In one corner of the hall was a curtained-off office for the manager, Mr. L. The word 'office' is the best euphemism possible. Maybe there was some office work done in there, but the main occupation was based round the camp bed in the corner.

Mr. L. was a fine-looking, tall young man who looked in the best of health. Why he was not serving his King and country was a mystery, but he did the next best thing by offering his services to the lonely wives! Mr. L's camp bed should have been awarded the George Cross for 'services over and above the call of duty'.

Everybody knew what went on behind the curtains in the corner but nobody said anything as it might just risk their turn! Apart from the 'office' Mr. L. organised all sorts of things in the 'communal'. He was like a chess piece dumped on a square to do his job and at the end of the game put back into the box. After the war Mr. L. disappeared and was never heard of again. I wonder what he told his children when they asked, "What did you do during the war, Daddy? Perhaps he told them he was doing secret work on the home front!

The main thing was the kosher kitchen which was in another corner of the hall. Mrs. Cohen was the cook and somehow or other she managed to serve up kosher food for those in need. Somebody must have brought the kosher food from London on the train. When there were parties for the children on festive holidays the Ladies Guild did the baking.

The armchairs round the room were always occupied by the same people sitting in the same places. Human beings in these circumstances appear to become very territorial about their sitting area and God help anybody who invaded that space. There were more arguments about chairs than about Hitler invading Poland.

In one of the corners sat Mrs. Marco huddled in her crochet shawl. She had emigrated from Russia decades before, but still did not speak English. Just after the war she and her two grown-up children moved into our back bedroom which was to cause many minor wars of their own.

Boba was a regular visitor to the hall and when she was not there the hall's visitors were at our house. At the hall they had to pay for their food and at No.12 they got it for free. I never remember the house without there being at least one visitor who had stayed for several meals – all served with chips.

To my knowledge my mother never set foot inside the 'communal'. She was much too quiet and reserved for that place. Basically she didn't fit in but her mother fitted in like Cinderella's foot in the glass slipper.

In the hall were the type of people she had grown up with, people from the east end of London whose parents had been immigrants and were only just out of the shetls of eastern Europe.

Boba offered a helping hand to all of them sometimes to her own disadvantage. Nearly all the 'residents' had nicknames because of their various characteristics. There was the 56er, a middle aged women who had accosted Boba in the street with "I know you, you're 56"! I never did know her name as she was always called by the nickname which managed to stick like glue.

One of the larger-than-life characters was 'Fat Becky'. You do not need a degree to understand why she had this nickname. She was huge to the point of being stuck in a taxi one day when she came to call at our house. She had a beautiful face, often the case with fat people and a body that did not reflect the hardship of war-time rationing. Strangely enough she was a favourite of Mr. L. and spent a lot of her war years behind the curtain in the 'communal'. It was a big curtain!

Becky had a heart as big as her body and everyone loved her. Somewhere in London there was an old weasel of a man who was her husband, but he was very rarely seen. She was probably only in her early thirties but from my perspective she was an old as the hills and about the same size.

There seemed to be a glut of fat ladies with tiny husbands, seaside postcard caricatures. I suppose the small husbands were not fit enough or big enough to be in the forces so they scuttled behind their wives and somehow made a living.

The language spoken in the communal was east-end London English with a large amount of yiddish. I came to love the yiddish language and though I understood it I was never very good at speaking it and I mainly prattled away in English. Understanding Yiddish has helped me out in all sorts of situations and have always been grateful for being immersed in it as a child.

One of the females that came regularly to the hall was Mrs. Lazarus, the medium. At the time she was about 45 with dark hair in a net rather like a Spanish dancer. Spiritualism is frowned upon in the Jewish religious world though this did not stop my Grandmother, Mrs. Lazarus and the aunts from visiting the spiritualist who practised above an optician opposite the castle. I was never taken so had no idea of exactly what went on across the road from the King and Queen.

In the hall there was often entertainments of some sort. Usually young girls doing tap dancing in tatty red costumes and scuffed shoes pounding out the dust from the wooden floor. The mothers loved it, of course, and nobody else cared one way or another. The pianist was sometimes my Auntie Dora, who played in time, and sometimes another lady who never quite got it together with the dancers.

Boba at these 'entertainments', always told the story of how she had lived in the same street as Jessie Matthews, the great thirties film star. "I watched her as a little girl in the street dancing round the market stalls", said Boba as if the glory of the girl's success somehow rubbed off on her.

I don't think any of the 'chorus line' in the communal hall ever got to the Hackney Empire let alone Hollywood. The little girls all had their dreams as they step-shuffled round the hall.

Being horribly shy I never wanted to be a dancer or anything else on a stage for that matter. Strange that fifty years later I wrote a musical show culminating with me doing a terrible dance in the last number. Perhaps I was right as a little girl and should never have gone on the stage!

The hall beneath the castle walls was, I suppose, a microcosm of the European shetl where everyone knew everyone else, loved them all and hated them all, and huddled together for warmth and security. My mother was too English, too retiring and really had nothing in common with this world. Why I did and she didn't is a mystery. Perhaps if she had sat amidst the dust, the laughter and the uncut moquet she might have been able to cope with her loss. But she didn't and her persona of an English Lady really did her no favours and somewhere along the line her roots got cut off and she only managed to stand alone in her little bit of the earth for thirty years.

The castle was just yards away from the hall but it might just as well have been on the moon. The community were eternally grateful to the King and to the country for their tolerance towards the 'immigrants' and no-one was more of a monarchist that Boba.

I doubt if many of the community were aware of the long history of the castle. A few, of course, may have been but it didn't play much, or any, part of their daily lives. The castle was the castle and the communal was the communal and never the twain shall mix.

Hopefully the castle will stand forever big, proud and solid, representing the long story of English history. The Jews beneath its walls have long since gone, but those surviving will never forget their time in the so-English of towns.

Windsor, with its winding river where the town got its name – Windlesora – means winding banks. Some of the wartime 'immigrants' have stayed in Windsor but the fingers on one hand would cover their numbers.

The Windsor synagogue moved to Slough at the end of the war – even that is gone today.

FOOD, GLORIOUS FOOD

Headless chickens performing their final steps in a *danse macabre* of death, were a common sight in our back garden. Boba kept chickens – but not for long. They were destined for the pot and the Jewish slaughterer, who never seemed to have a name except Shochet (ritual slaughterer), was called in to play the end game.

This dishevelled, long-coated, bearded man who must have lived locally but God knows where, would grab one of the chickens, haul it to the drain outside the back door and slit its throat with one slice of a sharp knife.

The feathered victim having received the necessary rites of a Hebrew blessing, would run around the garden headless until the last nerve ending switched off, whereupon it lay limp on the grass, ignored by its brethren who were later to meet the same fate.

Having paid the shochet, Boba would scoop up the bloody bird and with a sack over her knees in the garden, pluck the feathers until all that was left was the white skin specked with the stiff quills. These she burnt off over the gas stove. After an hour and a half of soaking and salting to make the bird kosher it was ready for the boiling pot.

How I longed for roast chicken, and 'all the trimmings'.

Our fowls were always old boilers whose main use was for the soup and not the meat. The flesh was mostly soaked away to get the goodness and the remaining meat was like human flesh that had stayed in water too long, soft and crinkled.

After the war the benighted chickens were taken to London to the kosher slaughter house and began their journey to the final chicken coop in the sky. What became of the schochet I never knew, but I presume he returned to the misty swamp from whence he originally materialised.

Next-door's chickens met their end with a swift twist of the neck and no blessing and no running around the garden – dead. As the years passed I hated the chickens and everything associated with them.

The neighbour on the other side without chickens had a beautiful manicured garden and I longed for ours to be just like that, smart and English. I wanted to be like them and sit in a deckchair with a cool lemonade and be a lady (something I never achieved).

Our garden, a euphemism for chicken run, was muddy, slimy and full of chicken droppings with skid marks. Boba, of course, didn't know about the niceties of fine gardens, chicken soup and eggs were all that mattered. For my part, food just appeared on the table and I wanted the meals without the mess.

The great food provider, chickens, had themselves to be fed. Mostly they were turned into cannibals by eating the leftovers of the rubberised bodies of their brethren. On other occasions they were fed with cooked potato peelings. When cooking, potato peelings have a smell of their own which can only be described as foul (excuse the pun). The smell pervaded the house and got into every crack and cranny like a warm swirling mist. How I hated those chickens and their dirt and their smells which invaded my life.

The other 'delicious' titbit on the chicken food menu was some sort of meal bought from the old chandlers shop in Oxford Road, Windsor. This shop came straight out of history and Cadfael, the monk from the Middle Ages, serving behind the counter would not have been out of place.

The chandler always wore a buttoned-up brown overall. Half-filled sacks with grain of all sorts, slumped their shoulders on the sawdust wooden floors. These sacks were near the front and as there was no shop window, the back of the shop was like Aladdin's cave.

I never penetrated to the interior of the emporium as I felt there was something lurking there waiting to jump out on me. What fascinated me was the adverts for Spratts Dog food. The name Spratts was written in different size letters to make the shapes of different breeds of dogs. I thought this was the cleverest thing in the world and I would stand outside the old shop reading the 'shapes' until Boba came out laden with meal for the horrible birds.

The chickens lost their control over the garden in 1947 when the Thames rose and they all got drowned in our dining room. Strange they should die on the dining room table where Boba had put them to be safe. Weird, like some sort of payback time, that the hens who died on the table where their ancestors had fed the humans, were not kosher and so could not be eaten.

With having the ghastly messy chicken we were never short of eggs, but Boba had a 'contact' in the local Co-op who supplied her with big boxes of dried egg powder. Everybody seemed to be doing a 'little business' with some sort of food in those years and Boba's was dried egg powder.

When a close friend called I would spy her going under the stairs with a ladle and scooping out some of the powder into a brown bag and handing it gleefully to the friend. What she received in return I do not know but Boba probably gave it away as she did most other things.

The other accompaniment to the soup were the noodles or in yiddish, lochen. No going and buying a packet from the supermarket during those years, everything had to be done by hand.

To make the said lochen Boba would fold up her sleeves and roll the pastry out on the table. Remember there were three people sleeping under that table, but no doubt they were out of their sleepy bowers by then.

Having made the pastry she would roll it out flat and then hang it up over the backs of a couple of chairs. There the limp pastry would hang until it was dry and ready for cutting. The next stage was to roll it into a length and chop finely into strips.

Boba managed to do this manoeuvre at tremendous speed and I would watch holding my breath praying that she wouldn't cut off the ends of her fingers. The speed was lightning fast and never even a fingernail was lost – at least I never found one in the soup!

Boba and the aunts were registered at the Co-op for their rations and I spent many hours in queues at this venue. The shop was large and the floor was covered in tiles and the tiles were covered in sawdust.

Built in the thirties it was a prime example of Art Deco. Not that Boba and the aunts realised that when they stood in the queues to be served the meagre rations.

All the dry stuff like tea, and Camp coffee was stacked on wooden shelves behind the long wooden counters. The bacon and fats counter ran at 90 degrees to the 'dry' stuff and all the assistants behind this counter wore white coats and long white aprons tied several times round the waist.

The queues were never-ending, mainly because the

assistants gossiped to the customers. The bane of Boba's life was a girl called Judith who never ever just served the customer without discussing the latest details of their lives, oblivious to the frustration of the folk further back in the queue.

How Boba loved the self-service shops that blossomed in the sixties before she died. Particularly Tesco with green shield stamps and large economy sized everything.

Once Boba and I finally reached the counter, over which I could just see, I was totally intrigued by Judith's tongue! The said tongue was a bright shade of purple because all the assistants had indelible pencils to mark off the ration books. Every time the book needed to be marked, Judith would stick out the purple tongue and run the pencil down the length of it to moisten the lead. This was to make the marking visible on the page. I presume an ordinary pencil would have been erased by unscrupulous customers wanting another ration either for eating or for selling (who would ever dream of doing such a thing!).

I would often hear of the words 'black market' and I imagined that all the things that were sold were black and emerged from a dark cellar.

How grocery shops have changed since the heady war-time days when sugar was weighed to the ration allowed and put into blue sugar paper. Judith was an expert, *pas excellence*, at twirling the blue paper into a cone and twisting the end to make it a secure venue for the sugar. I would try, with great determination, to fold paper into a cone but never accomplished the deed and just ended up with a wrinkled piece of flat paper.

Over at the fats counter we never, of course, had the bacon, but this did not stop me watching the paper-thin bacon sliding off the cutter. This machine was always presided over by an elderly man who used the cutter like a machine gun and probably dreamed of being a hero in the war he was too old to attend .

The greengrocer's shop was run by its owner, Mrs. Bucket. She was as one would have expected her to be with a name like that. A small wizened head topped an equally small wizened body. The body was wrapped in a fold-over apron which was constantly covered in potato dust.

The shop, like all the rest in Oxford Street, had the dirty wooden floor and dank interior. The vegetables appeared to be tired, particularly the carrots. Mrs. Bucket would scoop them up in the metal pan from the weighing machine as if they were prize exhibits.

Mrs. Bucket nearly always had a queue outside the shop as sometimes she would have some oranges and other rare goodies which Boba never managed to get. She was sure Mrs. Bucket was anti-semitic and would hide the precious fruit so she wouldn't get any.

"You wait", said Boba, "after the war you will have bananas and custard" which was like telling me that after the war the crown jewels would be mine. "After the war" was the phrase constantly on people's lips. Never having known anything but war, I couldn't imagine what "after the war" would be like. I suppose I thought it would be like a pink world where bananas and custard would be served at every meal and chickens would no longer exist.

Across the road from Mrs. Bucket was Stevens the baker, which was a heaven of wonderful smells and crusty white bloomers. Mrs. Turner had a cottage loaf and I always associated the front room with dainty slices of bread and the rest of the house with huge doorsteps of bloomer.

Mrs. Turner was able to cut the thinnest slices of bread I have ever seen even when she was drunk. Probably this was part of her being a lady! Boba, however, cut thick slices which went with her character of large generosity. She couldn't give a thin slice of bread to save her life. Of gentility she knew nothing, of love she knew everything.

Next door to the baker's was the wet fish shop which was Boba's paradise. The owner of the fish shop was Mr. Grub, which was entirely appropriate.

Boba would order whole cod, halibut and plaice and when she went to pick up the slippery fish the rest of the queue would gape at the old scruffy person carrying away such huge parcels of fish. Jewish people eat a lot of fish as most of the species are kosher and cold fried fish is God's nectar.

Every Friday afternoon Boba would stand frying fish to eat cold on a Saturday lunch time. Delicious is an understatement and fish has never tasted like that fried variety. We would eat the cold fish garnished with red horseradish which Mrs. King thought was jam. Boba would order whole fish and have a vicious time cleaning and scaling the creatures.

I felt sorry for the fish because without exception their watery eyes looked sorrowful, but this was no deterrent to the cat who would scoff the heads when they dropped into his feeding bowl.

I could never understand why cats loved fish, as cats, as far as I know can't swim, so where did they originally get their taste for water creatures? Sometimes Boba would boil the heads as an extra treat for the cat. Another atrocious smell in the kitchen. The world of today has lost a lot of smells, but I only have to remember back for the aroma to be there in my subconscience. Childhood is only a smell away.

Passover, the Jewish festival celebrating freedom, particularly from the Egyptians, was certainly no time of freedom in our house. The anomaly is that it takes about three weeks to prepare for the holiday when the original Hebrews left in minutes, not having time to let the bread rise. This must be part of the theory of the expanding universe.

Because these Hebrew tribes were released very grudgingly by the Pharaoh fed up to the back teeth with plagues, all orthodox Jewish homes go into overdrive on the cleaning front.

All the crockery had to be washed, dried and put away for a week while the passover crockery had to be washed, dried and taken out. At the end of the festival the whole thing had to be done again in reverse.

Our passover stuff was stored in a top cupboard in the kitchen and only saw the light of day during the special passover period. Boba had a penchant for good crockery and her Crown Derby 'pasech' stuff was her pride and joy.

Everything had to be changed, pots, pans, cutlery, tea towels. This is not straight forward as everything had to be divided into meat and milk dishes and the twain never to meet.

Boba could have sat in the black chair of Mastermind and answered questions on 'Orthodox kitchenware between 4,000 BC and 1944 AD. Why was it so important during the war when people were being slaughtered by the millions that the wrong knife didn't get into the wrong box? That question is answered, I suppose, by the fact that the Jews have survived every horror thrust upon them by this existence. Keeping up the traditions, the mortar of the bricks of faith, have pulled them through. The minutiae of living to a code which to the outside world may seem outdated and ridiculous, has given them a solid road on which to travel.

The big 'changeover' in our kitchen was particularly difficult as Mrs. Turner still carried on with her all-the-year-round saucepans, cooking her bacon and getting on with a gentile life. On top of this, life before the passover had to be accommodated using all the everyday things right up to the very last minute. Somehow all this madness was rather like a conjurer keeping all the balls in the air, with only one dropped ball to create disaster.

All came to a beautiful fruition at the passover supper (seder), which incidentally means order. These were magnificent evenings and I loved the 'Crown Derby' resplendent on the white tablecloth. The poor people in the camps starving for a slice of bread must have somehow fed their souls on the memories of seder nights held in the bosoms of their families and friends.

On the two seder nights our poor table was a match for any laid out in the castle in whose shadow we said our prayers and prayed for the freedom of our fellow Jews, slaves to Hitler instead of Pharaoh. Not only the name of the perpetrator of slavery had changed but the manifestations of evil had worsened.

The seder table was always crowded with the family and one of the uncles would read the story of the Exodus and half way through we would eat the symbols of the story. Karpas, greens dipped in salt water. The green is symbolic of spring and the salt water represents the bitterness of the people's tears. More bitterness with the horseradish dip and sweetness from the Haroset, a mixture of nuts, apple, honey and wine. The sweet dip represents the mortar for the bricks the Hebrews had to make.

The main dish on the table was the matzot which is the reminder of the unleaven bread that the people took with them into the desert. At the seder night the matzot is a special delight but by the end of Passover the euphoria had turned into boredom and loose bowels!

The story was stopped half way through for the meal, yes, chicken soup, followed by chicken, followed by boiled fruit.

Even though it was the ubiquitous chicken I loved the evening and invariably fell asleep before the end. The drowsiness was hastened by the obligatory glasses of wine.

One glass was always left for Elijah who is promised to be the forerunner of the Messiah. The door is left open for Elijah to enter and tell us that the Messiah is on his way. In my small mind God was always going to come via the train from Waterloo!

I always waited for Elijah to come and drink the wine, but he never did and as a mystical figure for children he is not a patch on Father Christmas who always comes with goodies! Elijah constantly failed to arrive and I eventually gave him up as a bad job.

Mrs. Turner was doing her bit by sitting in her room and knocking back the Rich Ruby which had not the slightest bit to do with Moses and the children of Israel. When I fell asleep at the table I was carried to my bed of two chairs in Mrs. Turner's room and for two nights of the year I was practically as drunk as she was!

THE RIVER

It was always there, constant, but ever-changing. The water had its moods sometimes matching my own childhood whims, but mostly going its own petulant way. This was an unrequited love affair, my love for the river and the river's indifference to me.

My home was fifty yards away from the waterfront and I spent every day of my childhood walking along the towpath observing the river through the seasons. You could never take the river for granted, for when it looked its most benign in summer it was at its deadliest. Its sparkling face face hid a black heart that stripped the lives of several swimmers each summer.

The summer, sweet summer, the river was full of boats and the skiffs of the Eton boys skimmed across the water. In 1940 nearly all the small pleasure boats hurried off to Dunkirk to bring back the soldiers off that benighted beach. One boat owner didn't go and he was forever afterwards a pariah.

The College chapel on the other side of the river, stood guard in small opposition to the castle. The Eton side of the bank was known as the Brocus. This was the venue for hopeful fishermen whose curses rang out as big boats sent waves bounding towards their lines, diminishing any hope of a catch.

Behind the anglers, tucked into the long grass were the lovers, entangled together like the weeds at the bottom of the river. These were the innocent days of the forties and fifties when the pill meant an Aspirin and good girls didn't!

These trysts were daring times snatched away from parental eyes when the heat of the sun warmed the young bodies and the long grass smelt like heaven.

A hand on a leg or the touch of a bosom were paradise found and the river lapped the bank in its own kissing time. Steamers pushed their way up the right side of the river like puffed up dowagers. The lesser craft of rowing boats and punts sidled away afraid of the large ladies with menacing boughs.

The cruisers that hired themselves out for 1/6d a seat chugged round the meandering bends to Boveney Lock, never to pass through the gates but to turn and return from whence they came. By the side of the lock was the white water of the weir, tumbling, whooshing and foaming into the still water.

In the early fifties at home when visitors failed to turn up on a Sunday I would ride the ferry from Windsor to the Eton side of the river. Tucked behind the legs of the ferryman as he wielded the long pole down into the darkness and up into the light again, rhythmic and smooth, I crossed the busy water. When my time comes to pay the ferryman I will know the fare and no doubt Cerberus will be a three-headed duck!

The 1d. fare was single so the return journey was by foot over Windsor-Bridge which linked Windsor and Eton, Castle and College. I don't think many members of the Jewish community ever ventured over the bridge to Eton because there was nothing there for them. The High Street consisted of antique shops, Eton College houses and lots of pubs. None of my family ever went there and Eton could have been on another planet as far as they were concerned.

Below Windsor Bridge were the Eton College boatyards where the "wet bobs" from the school would carry their skiffs shoulder high to the river. The single skiffs slid along the surface of the water, the oarsman bent over and heaving, the tiny splish-splash of the oars hardly audible from the bank.

Crews of eight pulled away full vigour from the landing stage, coached through a megaphone, held by a cyclist pedalling like fury on the bank. "Watch your right oar, Ponsonby". One two, one two". The coaches worked far harder than the oarsmen.

Just after the war the hoi polloi of day trippers would hire rowing boats for two hours. If you could fit the oars into the rowlocks you were considered river-worthy. Many a fine romance met choppy waters when young men in braces failed to impress their floral-frocked young ladies.

Creating waves and bobbing up and down were the elite of the river, the cruisers. Fifty years ago most of these were owned by blazer-swaggering 'captains'. They stood in the wheel house, steered with a straight eye and took themselves frightfully seriously. The wives invariable had blond hair, bright lipstick and never a sign of boat oil to mar their elegance. I envied these 'ladies', but never aspired to their positions.

On Summer Sundays the brass bands would play on an island in the river near my home. How we all loved it, seated on the banks watching the serge-uniformed bandsmen sweat out marches by Souza and softer music by Novello.

The mosquitoes had plumb picking but Boba and I didn't care. It was glorious, marvellous, summer would go on forever like the castle hanging up high above the river. I was stirred by the tunes, swept up with the warmth, the people and home was just across the road. The war was now over and life was one long thrill.

Late in the evening when the day visitors had departed Boba and I would walk along the quiet river bank, the white swans our sleepy companions. The water was black now. Gone the craft, gone the sparkling diamonds in the water, gone the lovers and the fishermen, just us to watch the night throw down its blanket.

Summer passed as all things pass and the falling leaves were the only craft to sail downstream. The captains of the pleasure cruisers gone to their boatyards to repair the ravages of the summer season. Only the swans, ducks and moorhens remained, faithful to their homes.

No visitors now, no boats, no ice cream, just the 'mists and mellow fruitfulness' of the river resting. Autumn always brought its own smells wafting across the water, bonfire smoke tinged with a hint of dampness.

Winter always came very quickly or so it seemed, bringing its own beauties. Clear blue skies reflected in the river, sharper than summer, late November fogs shrouding the water. All noise switched off, silent and still. Nothing but the slight slap of the grey water on to the bank.

No air, just Boba and me in the winter fog. I was happily scared. Frightened by a drip from an overhanging branch. Why did we walk this way home? Please God get us home safely. Really deep, deep down under the deep down I felt totally secure, as Boba was there clutching my hand and padding softly beside me.

The river pulls the fog towards it, attracting it, a siren with its slip-slop song. Across the water comes the bells of Eton College Chapel, muffled, dim, dead. Why did we walk this way?

The Alexandra Park railings across the road emerge as soldiers marching in a straight line from nowhere to nowhere. A red telephone box squirts out a bleary yellow light, a beacon, a sign that home is just a few more yards.

One year the river froze over and from nowhere emerged skaters. Brave, foolhardy folk with red scarves and black skates venturing on to the ice. Not me, no never me, for I had seen the river swallow its victims whole.

During the war I had watched transfixed at a soldier going down in the water with a full pack. The whole platoon was on exercises and the sergeant made them cross the winter water heavily laden with all their gear.

I heard as the young recruit pleaded with the sergeant not to make him go as he couldn't swim. The NCO was not interested and ordered the petrified boy into the water. He went down. They found a punt with a long pole and tried to fish him out, but the weight of the water with the full pack was too much and he slipped back into the water.

Three times they tried to hook him out and I watched horrified and transfixed at this death scene. They finally got him to the bank and tried artificial respiration but it was too late. His war ended there in the river with an audience and a sergeant too obsessed with the rules to care for a young boy who couldn't swim.

From winter to spring when the tides rose and the banks would regularly flood. In 1947 the spring tide coincided with the melting of the very heavy winter snow. Flood!

On Sunday morning the river was in swell, by Sunday night the water was rushing up the street, joined by the water coming from Maidenhead.

We had to move most of the furniture upstairs and bring the chickens into the house and sit them on the dining table. By Monday morning the river was in the house, half way up the stairs and punts were sailing through the front door.

Life upstairs must have been hell for Boba and the lodgers. There was nothing to cook on and poor Mrs Turner had never been acquainted with so much water in her life!

The street was an extension of the river and to get up to the castle area and shops you rang a bell from the front bedroom and a punt would arrive. Once on the punt which waited at the bottom of the stairs (the front door having been forced open by the rushing water), you were ferried up to an army-issue DUKW (an amphibious military transport vehicle or landing craft named from the manufacturers' code initials). Passengers alighted at the castle, did their shopping and waited for a DUKW to take them to the local punt.

Boba, of course, was worried about the chickens in the back garden. How could she stop the poor creatures from drowning in the rising water? The dining table had been left downstairs so the bedraggled hens, 14 of them, were brought into the house and placed on the table.

This was ironic to say the least, as most of the hen's friends and relatives had landed, dead and cooked, on the same table. Boba waded into them every day to try and feed them, but chickens not being the brightest of God's creatures, jumped off the table and drowned on the floor. When the water finally went down two weeks later all fourteen of the sorry birds had been drowned. We could not eat them, of course, as they had not been ritually killed.

As an eight-year-old I found this Venice-style living exciting. School had been abandoned and what more could a child wish for! When the water finally subsided Boba sent me away to relatives in London while the stinking mess left by the Thames could be cleared up. More time off school. Ever after the pink blotting paper felt damp.

The council sent machines to dry out the house and it was a long time before everything got back to normal, or as normal as things ever were at home.

I always loved the river, but I treated it with great respect because in most confrontations between the human being and the river the latter nearly always wins.

CAME THE RABBI

At the end of the war a large number of the Jewish population started drifting back to London to what remained of their homes. Pathe News at the cinemas was showing pictures of Belsen and the visions I saw have remained with me ever since. I was only six-and-a-half and I can't imagine why I was in a cinema at all, but the news came on and although I had no conception of what the images were they became indelibly stamped on my mind.

Rabbi Jacobovitch and his family departed from Windsor leaving behind a bereft congregation, shocked at what was found in the concentration camps and rudderless without a spiritual leader. Then came rabbi Baum.

He was a young man practically straight out of rabbinical school, full of religious zeal and a belief that God was more concerned with kosher food than what went on in Austwich. What the community thought of him I don't know, but coming after Rabbi Jacobovitz, anyone would have been second best.

Looking back over 50 years I wonder how any educated persons at that time could have kept such a naive faith. However, I suppose one must say that people still prayed as they were pushed into the gas chambers. They were no longer praying when they came out.

It must be said though, that the Jews as a people have only survived because of a strong and unswerving faith amidst the greatest opposition. Watery secular Jews like me would not have carried the nation forward and a great culture would have been lost. All the Old Biblical tribes except the Jews have been lost along the centuries mainly through assimilation. Jewish separatism has been its greatest asset and its greatest downfall. A secular Jew in Israel very angrily said to me, "These religious Jews are a thorn in our flesh". To which I replied, "If you pull out the thorn you will bleed to death".

Rabbi Baum came to our house because Boba kept the strictest kosher house in Windsor. He moved in like a King and proceeded to rule the house or, at least, he thought he did, with a religious rod of iron.

Everything had to be carried out strictly to religious code, particularly when it came to food and Shabbat observance. Rabbi Baum had God but Boba had gas bills with very little money to pay them.

For a religious Jew all work of any kind must cease on Friday at sunset and not resume again until Saturday sunset. Food has to be be kept warm on the cooker from Friday sundown until the first star out on Saturday evening. This meant keeping the gas stove permanently on for 24 hours and any electric appliances switched off. The radio, of course, was not allowed and Mrs King next door was called in to light the fire (mostly)!

Rabbi Baum went about his life firmly convinced that the food he ate on the Shabbat had been kept hot over night on a permanently switched-on cooker.

Boba was at least one jump ahead of him and switched off the cooker as soon as he departed for bed on Friday night and on again before he rose on the Sabbath. As soon as he left for the synagogue off would go the gas again. She worked on the policy of "what the eyes don't see the heart doesn't grieve over". She could never have paid the gas bills for such a regime and life went on unruffled. I don't suppose bills ever crossed the mind of the rabbi.

Any religious person reading this would probably be very angry, but there was no other way for Boba to survive. Most of life was compromise and hers was between God and the gas company and after all God never sent in any bills.

By anybody's standards Rabbi Baum was ultra-religious and expected everyone around him to be the same. Of course, the food was strictly kosher and Boba kept it that way however hard and expensive. One thing, about kosher food that is always certain and that is that it is always expensive.

For every different new forkfull of food Rabbi Baum put in his mouth there would be a separate prayer. For example, if we had chicken, potato and carrots there would be a nominated prayer for the three types of food. Probably by the time he ate the food it was well on the way to being stone cold.

At the end of the meal the grace would take at least 20 minutes. No-one would leave the table until the last Amen and on a Friday night we would all sing Hebrew songs for at least another half an hour. I used to wonder if God ever went to bed before we did.

Actually I loved Friday night when the candles were lit and the tablecloth was Persil white. The two loaves of bread crossed each other under a cloth and the bottle of wine reflected the candles on the table.

After the rabbi had blessed the bread it was dipped in salt and the pieces passed around the table. The bread and salt are representative of the gift of life.

The menu always consisted of chicken soup with noodles and or dumplings, followed by boiled chicken and vegetables. The sweet was mostly some sort of stewed fruit. As you were not allowed to have milk after a meat dinner, custard never accompanied the fruit. How I longed for custard and I am still a closet custard junkie!

We all wore our best clothes and it was really like the Christian equivalent of Sunday dinner. In most homes these days the whole family sitting together for any length of time is very unusual and I think a lot has been lost. Jewish families still honour the ritual of Friday night welcoming the 'Sabbath bride' with the lighting of the candles and the festive family meal.

Saturday was a long, long day. I was taken with the Rabbi to the synagogue metaphorically dragging my feet. He was so observant that he considered carrying a handkerchief 'labour'. Consequently he wore it round his neck where it constituted 'clothes' and not baggage. He certainly did not carry any money as that was an abomination on the Sabbath.

He wore black clothes and a large homberg hat and most of my time in the street with him constituted of extreme embarrassment.

Back home Boba was busy turning OFF the gas and switching ON the radio! She had no qualms about this as, after all, it was her home and Rabbi Baum was a very low-paying guest!

Saturday afternoon one was expected either to read religious texts or go to sleep. As neither of these options filled me with delight I would creep out and spend the afternoon with my non-Jewish friends. Where he thought I was I do not know because I didn't have a bedroom, sleeping. as I did, on the two chairs in Mrs. Turner's room.

We were allowed to go for a short walk but only a regulated distance. On one particular Saturday afternoon I slid out of the house to go with my friends to the summer fair on Eton College's playing fields.

The fair came annually to Agar's Plough, one of the college's fields, and all the local kids would walk the couple of miles from Windsor. clutching their shillings made up of pennies to spend on the rides and the games.

I had saved my money for weeks ready for the big day at the fair. I could hardly sit through the morning service, lunch and the interminable 'grace' waiting for the Rabbi to retire to his room. At last, at last, he trudged upstairs and I was just in time to meet my friends at the corner of the street for the tramp to the fair.

Boba certainly didn't mind me going as long as I was with some older children to keep on eye on me. She ruled her religion and not the other way round. My happiness was always her main concern. While the rabbi lay blissfully asleep in his room I crept out of the back door and fled down the street.

The fair was glorious, rides, games, loud music, roller balls, bumper cars and the divine horses going up and down as the turntable carried them round and round. Everywhere was brash colour and the ghost train would whoosh into the daylight away from the horrors inside the shack.

"I ain't never going on there with you no more", said one very dishevelled girl to her red-faced boy friend as they emerged into the light.

I envied the children who could go up on the swingboats and scream and shout without actually being sick. It was all a wonderland and a far cry from an afternoon of Leviticus and its rules. Fascinated I would watch avid fishers trying to lift a cuddly toy with a crane away from a very dusty packet of Players Weights. I never saw a crane actually lift a toy anywhere.

It took me a long time to part with my pennies as I first wanted to 'taste' whatever was on offer. I knew I couldn't shoot a diamond out of a playing card at fifteen feet or even throw a dart at a board so I saved my money for the hoops over fish bowls and rolling pennies down slopes. To this day I love the penny falls, but that sophistication was in the future.

Everything about the fair was heaven and it was the smells that seeped into my young being. The oil from the steam engines mixed with the dank odour of the wet grass and mud. It had always just rained and people's raincoats gave off an odour of wet perspiration. This was the nearest thing to my idea of heaven, so why should God mind that I spend my shabbat afternoon wondrously floating around this wonderland.

With my feet squelching in the soggy grass I bent over the boarding that surrounded the circular jars, home to the goldfish that swam in everlasting circles. This was IT. I was going to catch a goldfish bowl and have a pet, something I longed for and never had. One could never class the horrible dirty chickens as pets, when one ate them on Friday nights.

I passed my money over to the stallholder and he, in turn, passed me three ping pong balls. The idea was to throw a ball and get it into one of the empty bowls thereby getting the prize of the goldfish.

The first two balls failed miserably along with my childish hopes of a pet. But the third ball, that magnificent third ball dropped into a waiting bowl and I was a WINNER. Me, who had never won anything in my young life, had got a ball in a bowl and a luscious goldfish was mine, all mine.

I loved the little goldfish like crazy and I carried it around the fairground, clutched to my unformed bosom and spilling half the water down the front of my coat.

Time to go home and I left my friends at the corner of the street longing to get in and place the bowl proudly in the middle of the sideboard. Then I saw him, Rabbi Baum emerging through the front gate and walking towards me. How was I going to explain the goldfish, and from whence it arrived in the middle of the Sabbath afternoon? Goldfish didn't fall from heaven like manna, they came from fairgrounds and pet shops, both of which were dens of iniquity on Saturday afternoon.

Like lightening I dived into a neighbour's front garden and placed the bowl in the middle of the path and dashed out with empty arms to meet the rabbi a few paces away. "Where have you been all the afternoon"? questioned the black hat. "Just sitting by the river", I lied with hatred in my heart.

There was no way I could retrieve the fish as I couldn't explain it away and I lost my first and last pet that Saturday afternoon. I have often wondered what the neighbour thought when he opened his front door and there in the middle of his path a goldfish in a bowl had landed from heaven.

The only concession to the secular world by Rabbi Baum was the weekly trip to the Theatre Royal in Windsor. On Monday evening at the theatre the tickets were two for the price of one. That evening's performance was, in fact, the dress rehearsal for the current week's play.

There was a new play every week with the same actors which must have been like a treadmill playing in the evenings and rehearsing the next play in the afternoons. Boba and Rabbi Baum went to the theatre every single week. It was quite respectable for him to be with his 'old' landlady and I never found out if he or she paid for the ticket.

They must have stood out like sore thumbs in the genteel Windsor audience, he with his black clothes and skull cap and she with whatever she had thrown on that night. Boba and clothes never quite got it together.

More than resentment and anger the rabbi instilled in me intense embarrassment whenever he enrolled me in his extreme religious rites in public. It says in Jewish law somewhere that the dishes used especially for passover must be washed in running water.

The tap was not good enough for him, it had to be river water with all its nasties, that cleansed the plates for Passover. The two passovers he was with us he enlisted me to help him carry the crockery across the road to the river whilst he dipped them in the brown water. I would carry them over, bit by bit, and after he had slushed them in the foul Thames I would carry them back home ready for the next lot to be carted to the rabbi.

Unbeknown to him Boba was frantically washing them again under the tap to rid the crockery of the germs that infected the river at that time. There was an epidemic of polio at the time which was said to come from the river and here the rabbi was washing our dishes in the infection.

The worst part of it all, of course, was the embarrassment of seeing passers-by doing double takes at the sight of this black clad man in an homberg washing plates in the river and a child dashing backwards and forwards with the plates in her fumbling hands. Rabbi Baum did not know the word 'embarrassed', but I was the word personified.

Another terrible day by the river was for the ceremony of Tashlikh where it is customary to walk to a river, preferably one with fish in it, and recite special penitential prayers. This is accompanied by either emptying of one's pockets and casting the contents into the river. This symbolised the casting off of sins and beginning again.

Doing this in full public view was bad enough, but one year two of his wildly dressed chums in long black coats and sideburns arrived from London and I had to stand with the three of them by the riverside while they chanted prayers and emptied their pockets into the river.

I noticed that they had emptied their pockets of any

valuables before the ceremony! Perhaps the three men in 18th century Polish aristocratic clothes felt that their sins only amounted to a few crumbs and sticky balls of fluff and not to wallets and coins!

The ceremony has stood me in good stead in later life as nothing, absolutely nothing, including internal examinations, external examinations and having a baby, could ever be as embarrassing as those terrible times by the river.

Rabbi Baum stayed with us for two years and I was very happy when he left for a congregation in London. I learnt in latter years that he gave very good sermons, married, had two daughters and got divorced. Perhaps his poor wife couldn't stand his penchant for riverside religion.

On one memorable occasion Rabbi Baum took Boba and me to his father's wine shop in London. A modern marketing man would have dropped dead just stepping into that emporium.

It was very dark, gloomy and all the bottles were covered in dust. This was not the dust of vintage years it was just very ordinary, everyday, not-dusted dust. The bottles just sat on the shelves in seemingly random order.

I suppose old Mr Baum knew where everything was, but there was no way a shopper would know. Somebody must have walked into that Dickensian place and bought some wine as Mr Baum made a living.

I have the greatest respect for Orthodox Jewish ways, but I could never conform to them and am now a member of a Reform synagogue. Here Judaism is brought into the 21st century, but the orthodox hierachy feel we are watering down the religion. I suppose we are in some ways, but we are a Jewish home for people who cannot follow orthodox religiosity.

Maybe, just maybe the Almighty prefers the modern ways. On the other hand, as Tevye says, maybe not.

THE WHITE RUSSIAN

When the last aunt departed for home there was a hiatus of about 5 minutes (or so it seemed) before the new residents of the back bedroom moved in. The rabbi was in the small front room and Boba in the front bedroom. I, of course, was with Mrs. Turner in the front downstairs room.

Mrs Marcovitch, her daughter Sadie and son Mark became the new residents accompanied with dire warnings by Boba's friends not to let them in the house. Boba, of course, ignored the writing on the wall that this was a big mistake, and welcomed them with open arms. Boba knew nothing about closed arms and her open arms stretched across an acre.

The room contained one double bed, a campbed for Mark, one wardrobe, a cupboard, table, chest of drawers, one armchair, one upright chair and a gas fire. Into this room, 'marched in' as the army says, the new family.

Boba knew them from the communal hall where Mrs. Marcovitch (always known at Mrs Marco) sat all day crocheting doilies. Why anyone should have the need of doilies in the middle of a war is one of life's unanswered questions, but doilies in beige cotton came off the needle as regular as clockwork.

After the war ended the production of the objects carried on without a pause. What she did with these doilies I never found out, but presume she must have foisted them on unsuspecting persons for uses unspecified.

Sadie worked as a window-dresser in the British Home Stores in Slough. As far as I know she did that job all through the war so it must have been listed as a "reserved occupation". One presumes that shop windows had to look their best before they were blown to smithereens by a bomb!

Mark had been in the Pioneer Corps during the war and then worked as a tailoring presser in London catching the workmen's train every morning at 6.30am. Though not possessing an almighty brain he was friendly and affable and never complained about his lot. He was probably just glad to be alive.

Mrs Dora Marcovitch was a white Russian who, having survived the Pograms in her village, fled to England with her husband during the rule of the Bolshevics. They set up home in Mile End, East London and had three children. The eldest daughter had died some years previously, but was constantly on her mother's lips. Her husband also died prior to the war, but somehow he did not loom large in his wife's memory.

When the bombs started dropping on the East End, the family of now three, left their home and found themselves living in a tiny cottage in Eton Wick, a village on the outskirts of Eton. To get their kosher food the family spent most of the time in the communal hall.

Mrs Marco was tall, heavily stooped, thin with grey hair. The hair, parted in the middle had waves splashing their way back from the front of the head to the back. The waves ended in a bun at the nape of the neck. She spoke a very crippled English and most of the time her conversation was in Yiddish. The whole of her top half was always swathed in an all-encompassing shawl, crocheted, of course, The said garment was kept together by a large safety pin.

Sadie was about 35, tall like her mother, vaguely blondish hair, thin and very embittered. She longed to be married, but her longings never amounted to more then one-night stands and promises. American soldiers seemed to hover in her conversation.

The day they moved in it was like touching the blue paper, but unfortunately no-one could retire in the face of the blast. The two women, mother and daughter, were highly voluable and rows would blow up about anything and everything.

The old woman would shout down the stairs in yiddish, Boba would shout back at the bottom of the stairs and Mrs. Turner would sway along the hall in an inebriated haze to the kitchen. She could not understand any of the arguments and anyway, her friend, Rich Ruby, saw her through it all. These arguments all took place when the rabbi was out of the house tending to his flock.

Boba cooked, washed and cleaned for the new lodgers, and the new lodgers took it all for granted and expected more. Mrs Marco was a mischief maker and would cause trouble wherever she went. Hence the dire warnings from Boba's friends.

However, occasionally I would pop into the back room and listen to the old lady's tales of life in her Russian village under the Tzar. It was a living memory of Fiddler on the Roof and I would attend fascinated to stories of how the Jewish villagers would hide when the Cossack soldiers galloped through, spearing children with lances if one was in the way.

It was not all bad in the village and Mrs. Marcov relived for me the long hot summer days in the Russian cornfields watching the windmill sails creaking their never-ending journey catching the wind. She told me of the days she would lie just beneath the sails catching glimpses of the clouds through the wooden cross slats.

For all she had suffered in Russia it still remained her homeland and to where she would never return. Our local GP. Dr. Murrey, had been in Russia and when he came to visit they would speak the odd Russian sentence and that did her more good than the medicines he dished out.

The old lady suffered from asthma and she had a very early inhaler which was a big contraption with a black mouth and nose mask. The mouthpiece was attached to a rubber pipe leading into a ball which squeezed up the medication. She always called this her 'machinkie' and was forever looking for it amidst the heap of doilies.

My forays into the world of Tsarist Russia were nearly always followed by a visit to Mrs. Turner. The two women who happened to land up in the same house were poles apart. One who had come from the other side of the world and could hardly utter an English word and the other who had 'fallen' from the aristocracy and spoke gentrified English.

My grandmother stood between these two extreme lives and I didn't think anything was strange at all. I loved all of it as I was swept into a world of God and Golems in one room and Knightsbridge with thin bread and butter in the other. I didn't need a Tardis to travel between the two worlds, just a flight of stairs.

Every day at 4pm Mrs Turner held a 'tea party' in her room. Come sober or drunk the cups and saucers, teapot, sugar bowl and milk jug would be laid out on the black, papermache tray ready for the visitors. Boba was called in and then Mrs Turner would stand at the bottom of the stairs and summon Mrs. Marco to 'tea'.

The three old ladies would sit round the table with Mrs. Turner pouring the tea and making polite conversation. Mrs. Marco mumbling in Yiddish and Boba working out ways she could kick the Russian under the table 'by accident'. By the time of these parties my grandmother had begun to hate the old lady and wanted her to leave. Mrs. Marco was not about to leave as she was on a cushy number.

An observer looking at that room would have seen three very different old ladies drinking tea and enjoying each other's company. The truth was far from this and by 5p.m. they would have had an argument about something trivial and nobody would be speaking to anyone else until 4p.m. tea the next day.

One summer Sadie decided to take me on holiday to Margate, mainly as a cover for her 'assignations' with gentlemen of the military. Boba would have been horrified had she have known that I was left in the hotel of an evening while Sadie did her thing in Margate.

I hated every minute of being away from home and longed for the miserable days to pass. I was warned on pain of death not to say I didn't enjoy the holiday.

The Marco family received clothes parcels from distant relatives in America so consequently Mark wore funny suits just too big for him and resembled a tortoise just poking his head out of his shell. The suits had zip flies which was a marvel in itself and we all gazed in amazement at these new-fangled trousers. The Marco's were definitely in love with all things American, especially Sadie.

At this time the Marco's and Boba were all receiving National Assistance. Boba charged them rent plus a few shillings for the work she did for them such as shopping, cooking and cleaning. Of course, there was no such refinement as a rent book. Boba declared the rent money failing to mention that part of the rent included labour.

The Marco's reported her to the National Assistance, declaring that they were paying too much rent and needed an increase in their income. An investigation ensued and the Marco's declared that my grandmother had never ever done anything for them in the house and the money was just for rent.

The National Assistance took Boba to court for cheating them out of an amount of money which now escapes me. The Marco's were still living in the house and the atmosphere was horrendous.

On the day of the case, the welfare lady from the War Pensions Office came and took me to court in case Boba was sent to prison and I needed to be whipped away to a foster home. Of course, I didn't realise this at the time.

It was all so confusing for me to see my grandmother standing up in the well of the courtroom, a person on trial. It was even more confusing to listen to the lies the Marco family had told. I wanted to shout out in court that it was all wrong.

Of course, fortunately for me, I didn't realise that Boba could have gone to prison and that I could have been separated from her, maybe for good. I was used to the welfare lady being there as she often called just as so many other people called at the house.

My father's life had been estimated at 13 shillings a week, about 65p by today's standards. The Ministry of War Pensions dolled out this sum weekly to my grandmother to keep me in luxury! To see that the money was being spent properly and that I was being well brought up, Miss Hall, from the Pensions Welfare Office, came often to check up.

Thank goodness for a social worker who used common sense and did not judge the situation solely from a financial point of view. She must have seen and felt the love between the old lady and the young child and did not judge by the chaotic surroundings.

Boba must have dreaded these visits she knowing full well

what they meant. Miss Hall was always bombarded with a fulsome welcome and never put in an adverse report.

Later on when I went to the grammar school my reports had to be sent to her – I really can't think why unless they thought that if I was disruptive at school I would have to be sent to an institution.

My poor, poor grandmother had taken in these terrible people against all warnings and this was how she landed up, a suspected criminal who had defrauded His Majesty's government agency. Neither of her sons turned up to support her as they were both 'too busy'.

The judge took the word of the Marco's and did not believe my grandmother's true story of her working for them. She was found guilty. Sadie watched from the public gallery like a ghoul. Boba was fined £300 or three months in goal. She managed to pay the £300 with donations from friends and relatives.

Unbelievable as it may seem when we got back from court the Marco's were still in the house and were to stay there for another week before they finally moved out.

How Boba survived what had happened to her I don't know but survive she did and still carried on trusting and believing in people. It was only much later that I understood the full significance of what had happened.

There is an old Jewish tradition that when a dead person is taken from a house the woman of the house sweeps the front pavement to keep the dead away from the living.

On the day the Marco's finally moved Boba swept the pavement.

HARRY

If Uncle Harry had not existed Damon Runyon would have invented him. Harry Solomons was one of Boba's brothers and the odd one of the family. He came somewhere in the middle of the family and was totally unlike any of them.

He was by trade a presser which meant that he stood all day ironing garments in his father's workshop in the East End of London. This was by no means an easy task as it meant lifting heavy industrial irons for 10 hours a day. Actually, he hardly ever did stand all day as it took his mother half a day to get him out of bed.

Gambling was his obsession, horses, cards and anything else on which you could lay a bet. He was Jack the lad, sporting a smart suit, hat and cane and frequenting the seedy gambling joints in London.

Gambling was so much easier than pressing cheap garments and the rewards, when there were any rewards, were so much greater. He drove his parents to distraction.

When World War I broke out he decided that fighting for King and country was for idiots and not for people like him. He did not turn up for the army when his number came up and lived for the next four years in the attic avoiding the military police. I once asked him what he was doing in the

First War to which he replied, "Dodging it!".

Up in the dusty hideaway he would have card schools and play with all the chaps too old for military service. On one particular occasion he hung his jacket on a nail with a bundle of notes protruding from a pocket which was too much of a temptation for one of the card spielers. The money went and so did Harry in a blinding rage because it was impossible for him to report the theft to the police.

He married above him, way above him, a very clever immigrant girl from Russia. Hannah was a friend of his sister-in-law and had come to England hoping for a better life. This she did not get as life with Harry was one of have and have-not. One day a win and next day a loss.

Hannah was a pharmaceutical chemist and educated way beyond Harry and in those years, I suppose some husband was better than no husband at all. This was definitely not the case with Harry. No husband at all would have been a considerable improvement. They had one daughter, Betty, who made up in brains what her father lacked in sense and substance.

At the beginning of the Second World War they came down to stay in my mother's house in Windsor. They had the box room. How Hannah and Harry managed to live in the tiny room I do not know, but it was better than London's bombs.

By the forties Harry was a double for Alf Garnett from the bald head to the collarless shirt. He always wore a black opened waistcoat and his trousers came up to his armpits. His back stud was always in place, though I never saw a collar attached to it. From his waistcoat pocket protruded his glasses and his red ready-reckoner book – two essentials to Harry's life.

Harry was now too old for the army and he found himself a pressing job in Windsor. His fear of the bombs was intense and

The railway arch across the road in Barry Avenue which was converted into an air-raid shelter. Both ends were filled in and a door placed at the front facing the houses.

at the first sound of a raid he was the number one in the air-raid shelter. The shelter was across the road from the house in one of the arches that supported the railway line from Slough to Windsor.

At the first sound Harry, who somehow had the key to the shelter, would stand guard over the entrance, probably making a mental bet which 'plane would drop the first bomb.

Inside the shelter all the neighbours huddled in their night-clothes and wrapped in blankets. There were a few benches in there, but it always smelt dank. I suppose it also smelt of human fear, but at my young age I did not recognise it, but I knew the sound of the 'All clear' siren.

Mrs Turner had her special air-raid dress which she wore with a pearl choker and hair curlers. If she met her maker via a German bomb she was going to be well dressed and partially sober. How she thought she would release her ginger hair from the curlers before arriving at the pearly gates was information only she had!

Apart from being a gambler my grandmother's brother was a very humorous man. He was quick-witted and very funny and for all his faults you had to love his company. Everybody enjoyed being with him as long as he wasn't throwing their money away on a cert running at Newmarket.

The biggest bugbear of Harry's life was that "he couldn't get a bet on". These were the days before betting shops and street betting was illegal. The gambler had to find a 'bookies runner' who would furtively take your bet and pay you out should you have been lucky.

The local runner was a tiny fellow called Charlie Windsor. Everyone knew Charlie as you could see him every day hanging about outside the local paper shop in his long gaberdine mac and sometimes pushing his bike along the road.

From his mouth always protruded the remains of a tiny

roll-up cigarette. I remember him well, and although he was always pushing the bike I never saw him actually riding it and, for that matter, lighting up a new cigarette.

Harry and Charlie were pals and had regular assignations for the placing of bets and the paying out. The paying out was less often.

When Harry was not working, which seemed very often, his day was as regular as clockwork. First thing in the morning he would rush to the newsagents to buy a paper to check on the day's racing. I doubt if he ever looked at the front page in his life. Hitler may have been marching all over Europe, but what was running at Wincanton was far more important.

Having purchased the paper the morning was spent 'studying form' and no-one studied form better than Harry. He could have had a doctorate in studying form. Once he had decided on which sure winners he would place his bets, he would then have to go out to find Charlie.

Sometimes Charlie was not where he was supposed to be and Harry couldn't find him which was a tragedy as it meant he couldn't place a bet. A day without placing a bet, was, in Harry's world, a day wasted.

On the days when Charlie materialised, Harry placed his bet and then filled in time until the first edition of the *Star* newspaper came on the streets. Down to find Charlie again, who in his other persona as newspaper 'boy'. sold the *Star*, *News* and *Standard*, to buy the paper to check on the winners.

Should his horse have come first, second or third, Harry's next job was to work out the bet to ascertain what he had won. When it came to the complications of doubles, each ways, accumulators and various other complicated bets, Harry was the expert. He could reckon a bet in his head faster than any mathematician.

On one occasion I remember vividly he disappeared to the

toilet for a very long time. Eventually he emerged, downcast and extremely crestfallen. "What's the matter, Harry?", said Boba. "I just lost my ready-reckoner down the lavatory and when I bent over to pick it out I lost my glasses as well", replied Harry.

The soggy red ready-reckoner lay soaking in his hands, his pride and joy, his assistant with his bets, and it had just had the indignity of falling down the lavatory. Apparently he always worked out his bets sitting on the loo.

The rest of the family tolerated him and in a funny perverse way Boba loved him. Whatever anybody else would say about him, her replay was always the same, "Well, he's my brother and that's that".

He went back to London after the war and lived with his wife and daughter in a Nissan hut in the east end of London. I don't suppose these circumstances bothered him as he was completely oblivious to his surroundings. As long as the gee gees were running Harry was in heaven!.

SKOOL AND FINGS

Miss Bennett was a giant. At least in my three-year-old eyes she was huge and menacing. Actually I think she rose above the ground from her tiny feet to the top of her grey head, five foot, one inch – a veritable Amazon.

St Stephen's Primary School in Vansittart Road, Windsor, now in use as offices.

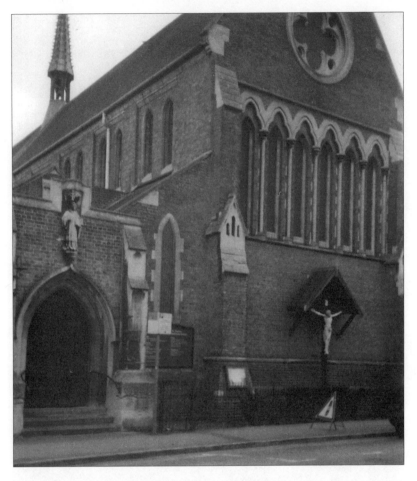

St Stephen's Church next door to the primary school in Vansittart Road, Windsor.

She was in charge of the nursery part of St. Stephen's School in Vansittart Road, just around the corner from our house in Barry Avenue. St Stephen's was a very high church and in the school attached to it, religion played a large part in the curriculum .

Clewer St. Stephen Junior Scho

WINDSOR

TERMINAL REPORT

Total Marks.....1085

Name.....Clare Mic'elson

Max. Marks.....1200

Position in Form.....5th

	MARKS				MARKS	
	Max	Obt.			Max	Obt.
Arithmetic ...	100	90	Drawing		100	95
English.			Handwork ...			
Composition	100	90	Needlework ...		100	90
Reading ...	100	100	Nature Study			
Writing ...	100	95	Phys. Training		100	95
Spelling ...	100	95	Divinity ...		100	95
Literature	100	85				
Geography ...	100	90				
History ...	100	65				

Remarks ..... Clare is a very willing worker, always ready to help

(Signed)..... Elsie H Kersley. Teacher.

..... Odingali Head Teacher.

Date.....27.7.50

My school report, July 1950, signed by Miss Kersley.

101

Why my mother, a fairly orthodox Jewish woman, should choose to send me to a very strict Christian school has never failed to amaze me. Probably for no better reason that it was the closest school to home. Looking back, it was the best thing she could have done as I grew up equally aware of both religions and a knowledge of the New Testament has always stood me in good stead.

A larger than life crucifix hung on the wall outside the church next to the school and I passed the figure every day without so much as a turn of the head. This statue had always been there and it was just part of the school. The smell of incense from the church used to penetrate my nose and I can never smell it now without I am back in St. Stephen's church. The longest word I knew was genuflect.

In 1942 Miss Bennett was probably hailing distance from 60 and she ruled her nursery domain with a rod of iron. The nursery was one very large room, with open doors at one end and a cloakroom at the other. The cloakroom was, in fact, just for hanging coats on low pegs and storing things, whereas the lavatories were in the playground. A large part of Miss Bennett's day was spent hauling wretched little boys out of the outside loos.

The girls' loos were also in the playground and were always cold, soggy and rather disgusting. We didn't think so at the time as the lavatories were an escape from the wrath of Miss Bennett. "Please may I be excused" was the get-out code for relief from the nursery day. Many a happy moment was spent secure behind the rotting wooden doors of the 'lavs'.

Miss Bennett looked like a petrol pump, a large square body topped with a round head. She always wore a flowery overall and her face was well-scrubbed and shining. Her hair was iron grey, parted on one side and hung just below her ears. The locks dropped in a straight downward projection with never a kink or curl to relief the monotony. I never heard her laugh.

How long she had reigned supreme over the nursery was a well-kept secret, but I am sure if she had been parachuted over Germany, Hitler would have surrendered immediately. I think she must have been the Allies secret weapon to be called in as a last-ditch stand.

There must have been about 35 assorted babes in the class, all of whom were jellies in Miss Bennett's presence. The mornings were spent learning to read which I found terribly boring as by three I could read – taught very proudly, by Boba's friend, Mrs. Adelman. Why she took it into her head to teach me to read is a profound mystery, but teach me to read she did.

My mother was alive at this time and I have no recollections of her reading anything to me. She did give me a copy of *Alice's Adventures in Wonderland* for my third birthday and probably expected me to read it myself.

I remember thinking how stupid the children were as they struggled with the letters of the alphabet while I read about the poor little match girl, the chimney sweep and other horribly sad stories. Lovable creatures like the Telly Tubbies were never part of my world.

After the limp sandwich lunch it was 'resting time'."Get your beds out children" boomed Miss Bennet which was the command to run to the cloakroom and struggle with a little green fold-up campbed, drag it to the large room and lie down upon it, feigning sleep. Mostly the time was spent feeling terribly alone and wanting to go home.

One poor child, Margaret Watling, would suck her fair plaits and cry all through the session. Miss Bennet managed to make the scene worse by calling her a crybaby and shouting at her to turn off the waterworks. Of course, she never did and rest-time must have been a nightmare for her. I just cried silently.

I would lay there just wanting it all to end so that I could go home. The only person that ever slept during those foul afternoons was Miss Bennet.

Just after lunch before the torture began I would stand on the steps of the nursery wishing somebody would come and take me home, but, of course, everybody at home thought I was having a wonderful time.

No child of three could have enjoyed that regime, and happiness came a very secondary thing to 'good behaviour' in those days. We were all too terrified to be other than well-behaved. Miss Bennet turned out over the years hundreds of little paragons who were really little broken dolls.

One day whoever was picking me up was late so I set off for home on my own, impatient to be away from the nursery. Half way home along Vansittart Road the air raid siren screeched out warning of approaching enemy aircraft. I had been told always to go to the ground in time of a raid and this I did crawling all the way home on my stomach. Even this was better than the time isolated on the green campbed.

I eventually moved up from Miss Bennett's class and I think for her it was probably a case of 'other people's babies', and retirement was her only escape. She is probably now in heaven petrifying the cherubs.

I moved into a class overseen by Mrs Marsden, the only married person on the staff. Unlike Miss Bennett she was kind and treated the children like humans. On one occasion she gave me a sailor doll which I dragged home by one arm and dumped when I got there. Dolls never interested me which was fortunate as I was never given any except the poor sailor who probably ended up in the bin.

Cold was the thing that entered my soul in that infant

school. I was always cold because, of course, there was no central heating and the only warmth emanated from the pot-bellied black stove in the middle of the classroom. In the nursery room, as far as I can remember, there was no heating whatsoever. The only heating came from Miss Bennet's lips.

My first encounter with the bulbous black stove was in Miss Balldock's class at the end of the war. My parents, had, by now gone. My father's death meant practically nothing as I only ever saw him twice when he was on leave, and my mother was replaced by my grandmother. The thing that really became of prime importance to me was the fire.

If you were lucky or favoured you were given a desk near the fire. I was neither and consequently my allocated seat was at the back of the end row where not an element of heat penetrated. Miss Balldock would squat on the fireguard surrounding the stove thereby blocking any heat that might have escaped my way.

My hands and feet were always full of chilblains which were painful in the cold and itchy in the warm. They only ever got warm at home when I would hold them inches away from the fire. The itching would then start and the evening would be spent scratching the swollen chilblains.

Mrs Turner would dab calamine lotion on the swollen and itching toes which gave a few moments relief. This is an ailment seldom mentioned these days and I wonder if any poor children suffer with them now.

I don't remember the lessons much in Miss Balldocks class, but I suppose I must have learnt something. The joy was to rush in from the playground and stand a few precious moments in front of the blackened stove before being told to get to my place in the nether regions.

Because St Stephen's was a church school our days always started with 'prayers'. All the classes assembled in the hall and the headmistress, Miss Wingate, would read the prayers and then we would sing the hymn for the day. The hymns were taken from the book *Hymns, Ancient & Modern*. By the time I left the school at eleven years of age I knew all the melodies and words practically off by heart.

The first lesson of the day was always Scripture and on Friday mornings Father Sheffield took a service in the church. He was called 'Father' even though it wasn't a Roman Catholic school and the Rev. Sheffield was married. Apart from his wife he seemed to have liked a little drink and often of an early morning Father would be seen loading up his little car with 'empties' – God bless him!

I was the only Jewish girl in the school, but nobody ever made me feel any different from the other children. I knew that Jesus lived at school and he never came home. Home was Yiddish and chicken soup, Hebrew and lutkes. School was Jesus, school dinners, hymns and Christmas. I was not confused or muddled because I knew where everything belonged and it never changed. I was as comfortable with the parish priest as I was with the rabbi and so it has remained for the rest of my life.

Miss Elsie Kersley was the most politically incorrect teacher you could ever hope to meet, and the best. She was the top teacher of the junior school and it was her job to get as many children as she could through the 11+ and on to the grammar school.

At 8.30 a.m. precisely she would alight from the local bus and sail into school like Cleopatra from her barge. A large bunch of girls (not me) would rush out, hang on her arms and escort her through the school gates and into the classroom.

She was about fifty, flamboyant and prone to purple clothes and Isadora Duncan scarves draped over her ample bosom. Her face was a mask of pancake make-up and the bright red gash of her lips matched the colour of her finger nails. The hair was 'touched up' and cut into small red curls rather like Medusa with worms. In her dress she was slightly more refined than a street walker.

Of course 'pc' had fortunately not become part of the wartime world and Miss Kersley ran her class like a never-ending competition. The desks were laid out in four rows, the front row being the elite position. The back row was where you landed up if you hadn't worked during the week and you spent the next seven days striving to move forward.

Every day after school Miss Kersley would spend an hour writing on both sides of the two blackboards our homework for the next night.

First thing in the morning it was our job to copy down the questions and endeavour to complete them that night. I learnt more maths, English and general knowledge from those blackboards than from anything else in my life.

Everything you did in that class, from putting your hand up first to answer a question, to dishing out the milk quietly, was marked. Following a correctly answered question Miss Kersley would bark, "Take fifty extras". This meant that you would have 50 extra marks added to your weekly total. This system speeded up your reactions as every mark counted.

On Friday afternoon Miss Kersley totalled everybody's marks for the week and we all moved places, either further forward or backward. I usually moved sideways on the front row. The top position was the extreme left desk looking from the front and I usually sat at about 4th place. I never ever made first or second, strive as I would.

In first place was a girl called Pearl Badger who, for some unknown reason, had been in Miss Kersley's class for a couple of years and was the teacher's 'pet'. We none of us resented Pearl as this was how things were and Miss Kersley always called her "My Pearl of great price".

I think Miss Kersley would turn in her grave if she knew about the "No child should lose, so no child can win" philosophy we have had in the education system.

Miss Kersley was a smoker and would often stand behind the blackboard for a cigarette. Why she thought we didn't know what she was doing was ridiculous, but she stood behind the board in case the headmistrees marched in and she could quickly douse the fag.

The smoke would rise from behind the board like Indian smoke signals, but so used to this occurrence were we that this was part of the school day.

Another time for a skulk behind the board was when her counterpart for the boys, Mr Barton, would come up for a chat. They both disappeared behind the blackboard and if we had been old enough to read body, or leg language, we could have done it then. From our desks we could only see two pairs of legs moving in relation to each other. The smoke would arise from the top of the blackboard and two pairs of feet would do the soft-shoe shuffle.

We never mixed with the boys because they had a separate playground once they were above Miss Bennett's class. This didn't bother us girls as we thought they were dirty and scruffy and of very little interest.

If Miss Kersley and Mr. Barton had an out-of-school relationship we never knew, but as neither of them got married it must have remained the excitement of trysts behind the blackboard.

Seventeen of us passed the 11+ in my year out of a class of about 30 which was good going and I owe a debt of gratitude to a teacher who gave me a splendid foundation of education and who, probably, these days would never be let inside a classroom.

The headmistress was Miss Wingate and she had her office half way up the main staircase. Two pupils from Miss Kersley's class were chosen to keep her office tidy and were paid the enormous sum of 6d. a week.

I got the job for a few weeks and I loved poking around the things on Miss Wingate's desk and 6d. was a super amount of money to me. The motto of the school was 'Think' which none of us understood at the time, but has come in handy in many a moment of crisis.

Boba who knew absolutely nothing about Miss Wingate told everyone that the lady was a relation of Orde Wingate, the great British soldier who had organised Jewish guerrillas in Palestine between 1936 and 1939. I am fairly sure that Miss Wingate was no such thing!

The regular visitor to the school was the 'nitty nurse' who pushed a disinfected pencil through your hair looking for fleas. We all hated her and hated her more when she found the dreaded objects crawling along your scalp.

Everybody had nits at one time or another, but it still felt shameful when they appeared in your own hair. When it was my turn to give lodgings to the tiny invaders I went home crying with a note clutched in my hand informing Boba.

Every night after then my hair was scraped with a horrid black comb to rid me of the foreign invaders. Boba was as determined to get rid of the nits as Churchill was to defend our shores. Finally I lived 'alone' but ever after when my hair was washed the comb made an appearance.

Although near home I always stayed for school dinners which were served in a hall next to the church. These school dinners lived up to the reputation of most school meals and consisted mainly of lumpy mashed potatoes and soggy greens. I suppose we were lucky to get any food at all bearing in mind the war and rationing.

Nobody at home gave a thought to the fact that I was eating non-kosher food in school and strictly kosher food at home. I also ate a lot with Mrs Turner and as I am not a ruminant the whole lot went into one stomach and God's wrath did not fall upon me!

After the war in 1950 the big prize for winning the 'scholarship' was a bicycle and the idea of going to the grammar school came very second to getting the longed-for bike. Boba, however, was not going to have any blackmail and I got my bike before the exam. This was very forward thinking and very much envied by my friends.

I actually owe the bike to Irving Berlin, the composer. A strange connection indeed at first sighting. A member of our family, still in London knew Irving Berlin's aunt who lived near her and the old aunt needed looking after for a couple of weeks following a spell in hospital.

The relation recommended a stay in Windsor as this was 1950 and the aunts had returned to London. Mrs Berlin arrived for the said two weeks and stayed three months thanks to the magnificent "looking after" by Boba.

Each of these weeks cost Irving Berlin, who was paying for his aunt, six guineas, a veritable fortune. From this largess came the wonderful, wonderful, bicycle and I took the scholarship knowing that the bicycle stood shining in the hall at home. Perhaps because I was not under strain to pass I sailed through with an A pass.

Boba knew less than nothing about bicycles but she grabbed her tatty bag, tucked it under her arm and marched me to Curry's to buy the bicycle. There it was in Curry's window, a black and white beauty, Triumph in make and design and it was going to be all mine.

It had slinky dropped handlebars, a sleek black saddle, a pump and glory upon glory, a bell. It didn't have any gears but it did have a dynamo lamp which was really something. The name Triumph was stencilled down the side and when Boba said, "We'll have that one", I was in love. No car has ever given me the thrill that I got from getting that bike.

I couldn't ride the thing so between us we pushed my Adonis home only to be greeted by our neighbour Mrs. King, who was a gentile and knew everything about bikes, (Jews knew nothing about bikes) with "She can't have those handlebars take it back".

Broken-hearted I went back to Curry's this time with Boba and Mrs. King to get a bicycle with normal handlebars. Fortunately it was still a Triumph and I was still over the proverbial moon when I pushed it home.

When Mrs Turner spotted the machine from her window she took it upon herself that she would teach me to ride! Hence, every afternoon after school I would wobble down the road and Mrs. Turner, nicely sozzled, would wobble along the pavement. The back streets of Windsor were not busy which was fortunate because every few yards I would fall off the bike and Mrs. Turner would fall on the pavement. We both picked ourselves up to continue our tortuous route, but learn to ride the bike I did.

Unfortunately Mrs Turner never learnt to stand upright for any length of time! Obviously Boba didn't think it at all odd that I was being taught to ride a machine by a lady who could hardly focus onto the road let alone her charge.

The world opened up for me with that machine and I rode it every day to the grammar school and later to college. Evenings were spent cycling everywhere with friends who passed the scholarship and got their prize. It got stolen one bonfire night and I was broken-hearted. My second bike was just a means of transport, not an object of love.

FLYPAPER AND GHOSTS

Mrs Lazarus, who was deep into the spiritual world, had a tragedy. Her son was killed riding a motorbike and she spent most of her time trying to contact him 'on the other side'. She had always been a strange woman, but her loss put her on the 'other side' of sanity.

To look at, Mrs Lazarus was the sort of person nobody notices. She was a brown woman, brown, thin hair, brown complexion and large brown age spots on her hands. Her body was average, about 5ft. 4ins. and her clothes hung from her shoulders as if they were on a hanger and not a body. Stand her in front of a brown door and she would have disappeared into it.

As there had been a son it is axiomatic there had been a husband, but one was never mentioned so presumably she stood alone. At one time she would turn up at the communal hall, sit in a corner and mumble. Nobody except Boba took much notice of her. She melted into the atmosphere.

For about a year she had been away in an asylum as mental hospitals were called in those days. Everybody felt sorry for her, but as far as I know, no-one actually visited her as anything to do with mental problems was shied away from in case the stigma attached itself to you.

One day, whilst I was hanging about in the hall deciding

which part of the house to visit, there was a knock on the door. This was a very common occurrence and I rushed to open it. On the doorstep was Mrs Lazarus with several bundles.

Coming up behind me, Boba invited her in and proceeded to make her something to eat knowing that she had escaped from the asylum and was on the run.

"I want to hold a seance", said Mrs. Lazarus with a mouth full of cake. "O.K, if that's what you want", said Boba, half placating her and half enjoying the thought of a seance in the house. Never one to miss an opportunity of excitement, Boba covered up the electric light shade with a newspaper thus making the room very dim.

The full flypaper looked like a shrivelled, rotting arm hanging down in the half light. Why do ghosts only ever come in the half-light? Perhaps they have poor eyes and can't stand the light!

My mother, of course, was out at work and knew nothing of what was going on in her house. Poor lady she was mostly unaware of what went on during the day.

The aunts and Mrs Turner were called in to the room, also Mrs Marco from the communal, who had popped in for egg and chips earlier in the day. The room was packed with all the assorted ladies round the table in the shadow light. I stood at Boba's side not knowing whether to be frightened.

Everyone in the room except Mrs Turner knew that Mrs. Lazarus had escaped from the asylum, but their curiosity overcame their fear and they intended to do what they were told in case Mrs. Lazarus turned violent. Mrs. Turner had, as usual, been imbibing the Rich Ruby and was past caring about anything. Her spirits were already coursing round her internal system.

"I want you all to put your hands touching each other on the table". This they all did except Mrs. Turner who had great difficulty in controlling her hands as they had a habit of floating upwards when the alcohol was in charge.

The room was quiet except for the heavy breathing from the participants and extra heavy breathing from Mrs. Marco who had asthma. I was transfixed by the happening and not really sure what it was all about.

"Now, all close your eyes and be very still and I will contact the other side", said the less-than-sane medium.

"I should put the cat out", said Boba. "Leave him alone, he has nothing to do with this" shouted the irritated Mrs. Lazarus. The cat stayed crouched under the table.

"Is anybody there? If so, knock on the table three times", intoned the medium.

Before the poor spirit had got its act together to start knocking, Mrs. Turner pronounced that she needed a drink and rose from the table on two very unstable legs. She swayed through the door to nip into her room to commune with Ruby.

Mrs. Lazarus became agitated which was not a good sign and Boba fearing the worst offered everybody a cup of tea.

"Shut up", shouted the medium. "You are upsetting the spirits".

On cue to the word "spirits" Mrs. Turner sashayed back to her seat fortified by Ruby's richness.

"Put your hands back on the table, please", implored a very frustrated and mad Mrs. Lazarus.

"Now, is there anybody there?" pleaded Mrs. Lazarus.

Silence. All that could be seen in the room were several pairs of white hands, a floating one from a returned Mrs. Turner and the large flycatcher slightly oscillating.

Suddenly a screech from Mrs Marco.

"She's fallen into a trunk. She's fallen into a trunk".

What she meant, of course, was that Mrs. Lazarus had fallen into a trance and was mumbling words nobody could quite hear. All ears and eyes were concentrated on the medium waiting to see if there was a "message" for them. There is nothing more selfish than people at a seance. They are not the slightest bit interested in other people's messages, only words of comfort from their passed-on loved ones is all that matters.

"Where are you, Ronnie?" Are you there, my Ronnie?" Ronnie the ghost with that unlikely name did nothing. In the world of the spirits I would assume that anyone with the name of Ronnie would be very much down the pecking order from Ann Boleyn and other such notables, consequently keeping a low profile. Apart from that, what self-respecting ghost admits to having a mad mother.

Mrs Lazarus was again calling to her son when from Mrs. Marco came an almighty screech. The occupants of the room in one voice (except me and Mrs Turner) shouted "Oh vey" which is the yiddish phrase for everything bearing anything resembling a disaster.

The reason for the screech was the cat which had jumped up on to Mrs. Marco's lap and got itself caught in her all-enveloping shawl. The poor thing was petrified because the more it struggled to release itself the more it got entwined. In the half light it appeared as a writhing black mass with several dozens arms and legs.

Mrs Marco struggled and wheezed trying to extricate the monster from her shawl and the more she flayed her arms the worse the cat became. The old Russian whirled herself around like a dervish and I expected the cat to come flying across the room at any moment.

Boba recognised the problem, left her place at the table and tried to untangle the animal. The room disintegrated into a cauldron of shrieks, shouts and frightened sighs. Mrs Lazarus was oblivious to it all still calling to Ronnie who failed to materialise.

Mrs. Turner's hands took on an agitated life of their own floating a foot above the table with their owner failing to keep them in place.

In the midst of this melee there was a knock on the front door. The usual stupid question of "Who's that?" came from one of the aunts fearing it would be the Rabbi. Leaving the monster in Mrs. Marco's lap my grandmother went to answer the knocking.

On the step were two unknown gentlemen enquiring if Mrs. Lazarus was in the house. The men were from the asylum who had taken most of the day trying to track down the missing patient. They had tried a large proportion of the Jewish homes in the town. None the residents, of course, had seen her, and recommended that they tried our house which was where most of the odd balls of the area turned up at one time or another.

My grandmother with her usual "Come in, come in, she's here" led them into the hall. The aunts came out from the room rather sheepishly and disappeared quietly into various other parts of the house.

Mrs. Marco had freed herself from the black cat and was taking deep breaths into her asthma machine. The floating hands of Mrs. Turner led her back to her room for a needy commune with the other spirits. Mrs. Lazarus was oblivious to it all, still in her trance and still trying to contact Ronnie.

I, of course, was loving it all as I really understood none of it and as long as Boba was around all was fine in my world. Strange happenings were all part of my everyday life and there was no real norm. Everything in this topsy-turvy world was part of my life to be savoured and enjoyed.

The men finally managed to wake Mrs. Lazarus and she was led away never, as far as I knew, to be heard of again. Poor lady. Of Ronnie there was no sign.

MINDING THEIR OWN BUSINESS

When the ritual slaughterer left Windsor immediately after the war, we were left with the feathered monsters and no way of getting them killed ritually for the table. The answer to the problem was to go to London with a live chicken and come back with a dead one having visited the Jewish slaughterhouse in the East End.

The cheapest way to get to London was on the 'workman's' train on the old Southern Railway from Windsor Riverside to Waterloo.

Boba had invested in a cockerel for breeding purposes, but he only lasted two weeks. Neighbours were not enamoured with his early morning call and verbally made their feelings known. The cockerel had to go.

Going meant that I was awakened at 5 am to stumble about the freezing house, ashes dead in the grate and newspapers carpeting the floor, to get ready for the train. However, first we had to catch the crowing cockerel, no easy task in the morning darkness.

Slipping about the dark garden (chickens manage to make very slippery messes everywhere) Boba and I finally located the bird. Trouble was he spotted us at the same moment and was off amidst a fluttering of wings and loud squawks.

The shrieks woke his 'wives' and the sleeping neighbours and I wondered that Boba thought the chickens might respond to her "Shh, you'll wake the neighbours." As far as the neighbours were concerned it was too late.

Up and down the terraced row of houses the lights flashed on and heads popped through windows. Undaunted by the threats of neighbours to send for the police and other nasties, Boba at last managed to catch the doomed bird. I stood by with the big black funereal bag in which he was to make his last earthly journey.

Neighbouring lights dimmed one by one and the old lady, child and cockerel crept through the approaching dawn to the railway station. Lined up on the platform were the commuters – city gents to a man.

A veritable army of bowler hats, striped trousers, black jackets and obligatory umbrellas stood to attention waiting for the train. Into the midst of the brigade marched one old lady in a long, threadbare maroon coat, headscarf and brown, splayed, flat shoes accompanied by a raggety child holding up to its chin by two handles, one big, black moving bag.

Of the black army not a head jerked, not a muscle moved, not an eyelid fluttered. This Windsor army knew that if one ignored such creatures they would eventually go away. These creatures from another world were not about to go away, they were actually going to get on the train.

Windsor Riverside station is a terminus and the train was always in position and it only needed a signal from the guard for the rush to the seats to begin. Guard's arm up and immediately manicured hands reached for the brass door handles and the carriages were besieged.

Undaunted Boba, who had no respect or awe for bowler hats or briefcases, muscled her way into the carriage, dragging me and the bag behind her. The old-style carriages were without a corridor and were simply two benches facing each other with about a foot between the knees of either side.

Boba and I settled down facing each other squashed between the faceless men. They never had faces because they disappeared behind broadsheet newspapers. At my tender age the newspapers looked the size of sheets.

The bag was now between my feet and I could feel the warm contents scrabbling about the bottom. From behind the papers our fellow travellers could see nothing. I studied the sepia prints of Sidmouth, Folkstone and Dover framed above the bench opposite. The places all looked exactly the same, with dreary 1930's people sitting on boring beaches with a pier in the background. My association with English seaside resorts has always been of brown depression.

With the steady diddly-dee, diddly-dum of the train wheels my bag settled itself down, then just outside Staines it happened – the train jerked, the handles parted and the cockerel spied its first bit of daylight.

The crow that emanated from that bag has stayed with me forever. I was ready to die, the humiliation, the embarrassment. I wasted my feelings for as I opened my tightly shut eyes I saw all the papers still in place. Not a page turned and not a shocked face emerged. I thought I noticed one foot twitch. No way could a cock crowing on the 6.02 am train to Waterloo be normal, but to those men in the carriage it was just to be ignored.

Boba did her stage whisper yiddish telling me to put the handles together and plunge the wretched bird into darkness. I was not able to manipulate the handles quickly enough before the cockerel crowed again. The one in the Bible crowed three times, twice was enough for me.

The rest of the journey passed in comparative quiet with my knuckles getting whiter and whiter as I tightly clasped the handles of the bag. Waterloo finally arrived seemingly after a decade, and I jumped up to get out of that prison first.

I looked to neither left nor right as I spilled onto the platform clutching the evil bag. My hands were now numb and my knuckles white as they clasped the handles together. Undeterred and unabashed Boba made her way out between the black ants, saying good morning to blank-faced replies. How could she?!

Once on the platform I flatly refused to carry the bag another inch and handed it over to Boba manipulating the handles so they didn't part and instigate a crow. I walked ahead of my grandmother, she wasn't with me and I certainly didn't know her!

We caught the 76 bus to Liverpool Street, the route for the slaughterhouse. The bus ride passed without any crowing, but I once more had to hold the bag whilst Boba scrabbled in her handbag for the fare.

Trying to hold onto a moving bag and appear nonchalant was beyond the capabilities of someone like me. Boba wasn't bothered, moving bags were the everyday norm as far as she was concerned.

Each time the bus bell dinged the cockerel jumped accompanied by me as by this time the bag was sitting on my lap. If only someone had spoken to break the atmosphere, but they didn't, minding their own business as only the English can.

Off the bus at last, we made our way through the early morning bustle and smell of Petticoat Lane to the Jewish slaughterhouse. The 'death house' was noise, stinks, blood, feathers, blood splattered white tiles and sweaty human beings.

The main happening was to hand over your bird amidst squawks, to the bearded, aproned slaughterer, who would say a prayer whilst slitting the animal's throat. I always hoped the condemned bird sincerely appreciated the prayer!.

Kosher meat has to have the blood drained away, so once the deed had been done the fowl would be stuck head down in a hole in a white tiled trough. The trough was like a huge cribbage board with holes at intervals along the top where the head would be stuck for the blood to drain away. The legs stuck in the air like dying can-can dancers.

This ceremony completed, the bird would be handed back, money exchanged and the owners of the now bloodless creature would make their way up the stone stairs to the chicken pluckers.

In Jewish hierarchy a rabbi is at the top of the ladder closely followed by doctors, solicitors and accountants. At the bottom of the ladder come the chicken 'flickers'.

These 'ladies' would sit on low boxes amidst piles of feathers with their ample lags apart, and pluck the dead birds. Over their laps were blood-stained sacks and often the remains of their pickled herring lunch.

These ladies were in competition, and as soon as a customer walked through the door screams would assail them for the job of plucking the chickens. Between screaming they cursed each other and the air was not only thick with feathers but bad-mouthed rhetoric. The women would have sat around the guillotine in Paris quite happily plucking instead of knitting. They frightened me to death.

Our cockerel landed on the nearest lap and within minutes he was naked. Stripped of all his pride he lay limp and impotent. His cocky strut gone and fine coxcomb pale and droopy he fell with a flat thump at the bottom of the black bag. On top of him in a thick brown paper bag were his feathers, destined for a pillow, an ignominious end.

Following a visit to Bloom's saltbeef shop for a hot saltbeef sandwich, we made a tour of the various relatives living back in the area. These were the aunts who had returned from whence they came after the war.

One special place to be furtively visited was Fox's chemist shop which sold the hair restorer that Boba used. Goodness knows what was in the brown bottle but it seemed to keep back the grey for several years. Eventually Boba could no longer fight the battle of the grey and Fox's Hair Restorer was no longer to be seen in the house. Funny for a woman who was a disaster with clothes to be so concerned about her hair.

Waterloo, platform 19, at 6pm. we waited for the train home to Windsor. The bowler hats who had seen us in the morning hurried away down the platform.

On the train with the black bag immobile and quiet, I felt happy. I helped Boba lift the bag on the 'knotted' rack above the sepia prints (now changed to Bognor, Bournemouth and Poole) so the standing passengers would have more foot room. Contented I curled up in the corner seat, nose pressed against the filthy window.

The carriage was packed with commuters returning to all stops to Windsor. We were off, the standing gentlemen even managing to read their folded-up evening papers. Richmond, Twickenham, Ashford, Feltham. Calais may be printed on Mary Tudor's heart, but Feltham is printed on mine.

We had just passed Feltham when the owner of the brief case-next to our bag decided he wanted his possession off the rack. Standing up his hand pulled at the leather handle of the briefcase, dislodging our bag and pulling it to the edge of the knitted cradle.

The flimsy paper bag hung over the edge of the rack gorging out its feathery contents. Down, down, down they came like snowflakes, gently covering black hats, jackets, overcoats, moustaches, hairdos, papers, noses, eyebrows and everything. Large feathers, small feathers, spikey feathers, bloody feathers, all came fluttering down in the silence.

One stuck to the toecap of a polished shoe, its owner staring fixedly at the floor. At last the commuter dolls came to life blowing the feathers in all directions. The carriage was in pandemonium, arms flaying and lips pursed in an endeavour to keep the feathers at bay. Of course, nothing could help, the feathers fluttered down and rested where they will. There was still half an hour to reach Windsor and Boba was making things worse by trying to collect the feathers from where they had landed.

I had reached the point beyond embarrassment and could quite happily have thrown myself out of the door onto the speeding track. Eventually we pulled into the station and our fellow travellers looking like animated chickens quickly rushed down the platform. What story the commuters told their wives as to how they came to be covered in feathers must be left to the imagination.

Once more the chickens had blighted my life. Boba, of course, thought it was funny. That was the very last time I agreed to go to the slaughterhouse.

I GAINED A BROTHER

Its a long way from a small village, Chodecx in Eastern Europe to the very English of towns, Windsor, particularly when you have come via Auschwitz.

Roman Halter had made that journey in 1945 when Britain agreed to take in one thousand young survivors of the Holocaust. Only 732 could be found and these boys and girls were flown from Prague and Munich to Windermere and Southampton. Known as 'The Boys', these children created a family of themselves and shortly after Roman arrived in the UK my grandmother opened her door and her heart to him.

The historian Sir Martin Gilbert has written a book called *The Boys, Triumph Over Adversity* recounting the stories of these youngsters.

At last I had found a brother and he a sister, not to replace those he had lost in the Holocaust, but a new and close relationship.

He was a young man of about 16, tall, slim with blond wavy hair and he was my hero. How could one not love such a person. For someone who had been to hell and back many times, he seemed to me to be always smiling. Of course, at the time I knew really nothing of his background so our relationship was not clouded, on my part; by fog of ghastly ghosts. To me he was the brother I never had.

Roman had many talents and one of them was swimming. He joined the Windsor Swimming Club and was held in great affection by the other members, not only for his great swimming ability, but for his general demeanour. He regularly swam in the Lock to Lock (Boveny to Romney) race which is about 3 miles and a great achievement.

Boba was vastly proud of this young man and on one occasion she stood on the riverside using her full force of lung power to cheer him on to win the race. Such was her enthusiasm that in mid-cheer her false teeth left her mouth and sunk to the bottom of the Thames.

After an exhausting swim which, in fact, he won, the poor young man had to do several dives in the murky river to retrieve the teeth. Passing fish must have thought there was a new evil predator ready to chew them up in its frightening jaws!

Boba was always urging me to get Roman to teach me to swim. He was anxious to do so but I would never go as I had a dislike of the water. "You'll regret it, one day", admonished an angry grandmother and never was a truer word spoken.

What Roman did to was to teach me to play chess and also to appreciate good books. I remember so well him reading Homer's *Odyssey* in his slightly broken English. This was really 'a book too far' for an eight year old, but I have never forgotten it.

Boba lavished a lot of love on her new 'baby', but sometimes her reading of a situation was not always correct. As a child Roman had come from a good family who taught the children proper table manners. Roman had been told never finish off all the food on your plate, leave a polite piece at the end. Boba interpreted this as having given him too much food never having been schooled in etiquette of any sort!

To remedy the situation she put less on his plate, but he still left food behind. The amount of food became less and less and both Boba and Roman could not sort out the problem as neither wanted to mention it. However, Roman had had enough of feeling hungry during the war and finally told my grandmother why he was leaving food on his plate. Forever after his plate was loaded to capacity!

The 'Boys' needed a meeting place where they could gather and strengthen their 'family' ties. To this end the Primrose Club was opened in July 1947 at 26/27 Belsize Park, West London. The club was named the Primrose Club after the local telephone exchange.

Often Roman took me to the Primrose Club and the boys indulged the little girl by playing table tennis with her. To me this club was the height of excitement with lots of young men and women around laughing and having fun. The little girl had no idea of the cumulative evil these young people had encountered in their early lives.

Unlike the rest of this book, this chapter is about what has happened rather than what did happen. To me, my 'brother' is a success story against all the odds. How the human spirit has overcome the worst that mankind over the centuries has thrown up.

When Roman left us he trained to be architect and ran his own practice. He married Susie, a champion swimmer from Hungary and had three children. When the responsibility of bringing up a family had passed Roman gave up his practice and started to work on stained-glass windows and armorial designs for buildings.

The holocaust has been portrayed in many of his paintings and he has become a very highly regarded artist, particularly in the Jewish world. His stained-glass windows adorn synagogues and public buildings. Roman's work is also at Yad

Vashem, the Holocaust memorial in Jerusalem and at Beil Lohamli.

He has worked extremely hard for justice for the German Slave Labour compensation with his friend, Rudy Kennedy, another survivor. Roman was a slave labourer in Dresden and knows too well why the Allies bombed the city.

His swimming still plays a large part in his life and Susie swims all over the world in the older-age bracket.

My only sorrow is that Boba is not alive to see Roman now, for his memories and heartache have not gone away.

"Clare, things do not get better with time, they get worse", Roman confided in me.

Some of his terrible memories have been videod in the form of a talking head and can be seen at the Holocaust Exhibition at the Imperial War Museum in London. There are other talking heads at the Exhibition and they all tell their individual stories of when the world went mad.

Roman and I have kept in touch over the years and we always celebrate our special family and working moments together. I may not have had a 'birth brother' but I had one that came for a while and stayed for a lifetime.

BOBA IN LOVE

Whoever said that love was for the young? Boba, of course, fell in love at 65. Her 'in love' was totally different from her loving which was in operation at all times. Her being 'in love' was reserved for the most unworthy character that ever drew breath.

Roger Cooper was a womaniser, a cad, an ingrate and one of the most handsome men ever to walk this earth and she loved him. With love like that there are no questions and still less answers. At the time, of course, I didn't understand it, that would come later.

The ghastly Marco family had moved out and the back room was vacant – but not for long.

How he knew the room was vacant I do not know, but he turned up one day out of the blue and rang the bell. Boba opened the door to this magnificent vision of 6ft.4ins. with blue eyes, light brown hair and creases in his trousers that could cut hard cheese. He smiled at her and the years fell away. She was 18 again and proceeded to act like it.

Her light was lit and from that moment on he could do not wrong, though of course, he did and magnificently. The more she loved him the more I loathed him with a vengeance.

Of course, this was not a physical relationship and the love was only on one side. For Boba he needed only to walk through the door and her eyes lit up like a lighthouse beacon in a storm.

The thing with Boba was that she liked handsome men. She had married one though he had been a decent human being. Roger (not his real name) was positively indecent though Boba only saw what she wanted to see in this young Adonis.

Roger was about 27 when he walked into our lives. He had been cashiered out of the Household Cavalry for having seduced an officer's wife. Probably she had not needed much seducing, but Roger left the guards regiment with a large stain on his army record.

Not to be deterred he became, what else, an estate agent which was a job made in heaven for him. As the saying goes, he could charm the birds off the trees and also gullible women into persuading their husbands into buying unsuitable houses.

Roger's background was a mystery and over the several years he lived with us we found out nothing about him except he had a mother tucked away somewhere. He never wrote or received letters and as we were not on the 'phone he made no contact with any other world.

I suppose he must have been a con man with all the charm and chat that the job needed. To give him his due he always paid his rent and never tried to dupe my grandmother financially. He had other ways of twisting her round not only his little finger, but the rest of his hand.

The more she adored him the more I hated him and he reciprocated. In the whole of my life nothing and nobody had come between my grandmother and myself. Suddenly this man had taken my place and I detested him for it.

Of course, his looks, his sparkling laundered shirts, stiff collars and fine tailored suits meant nothing to me. I knew he used my grandmother and she couldn't see it. I was about 10 at this time and old enough to see him for what he was.

I refused to talk to him which did not bother him in the slightest. As far as he was concerned I was just a very silly kid who was not even worth charming.

On one occasion when we had a row he told me that I was so awful that no man would ever look at me and I would remain an old maid. This did nothing for my confidence as I felt very much an ugly duckling anyway.

Roger did three things with his life, sold houses, charmed my grandmother and made love to lots of women. He found all three very easy.

On one occasion he told Boba that the Doctor said he needed to go on a diet because of a skin condition. The diet consisted of tinned salmon and other such delicacies which she duly dished up at great expensive to herself. She only cared that she pleased him.

He fascinated her and he made her feel young and wanted and now I can understand it, but not then. At that time I only wanted him to move out which he did one Friday only to move back on the Monday! Probably the woman he was going to live with came to her senses after one weekend.

This man-about-town drove a vintage car of the type gangsters drove in the twenties. There were even bullet holes in the back window, whether they were real or not I do not know. Naturally he had to have a car like that as a Morris Minor would have hardly have suited his image.

He went out every night, goodness knows where and would often come home with trophies connected with the evening. One such trophy was a pair of very small knickers which he threw out of his bedroom window and which Boba proceeded to find on the grass the next morning. Presuming they had blown over from next door she kindly went and pinned them back on the neighbour's washing line.

The said neighbour bewildered how these knickers came to be on her line, promptly pinned them on her neighbour's line further up the street. The frilly garment travelled up and down the road for several days!

On one horrible occasion he went to visit a girlfriend who was in hospital for an appendix operation. Visiting at the same time was her mother whom he kindly offered a lift home and proceeded to bed her seemingly to the glee of the lady concerned. For months afterwards, according to his tales to Boba, he juggled between the two ladies and eventually, of course, got found out.

The only thing I can thank him for is an appreciation and love of traditional jazz. He had a large collection of 78rpm. jazz records which he would play whenever he was home. One of the songs played was true in my case, *I'll be glad when you're dead you rascal you.*

I would pretend to be oblivious to his stories and though I did not understand them fully I more or less got the picture. What I didn't understand was why a woman with religious convictions, who entertained rabbis at her table, could be fascinated by this man. In love there is no rhyme nor reason.

At ten I was too young to understand but I am sure many a mature lady might feel the same. How true that love is blind and even after he had finally gone Boba never really got her sight back where he was concerned. Never let it be said that any age is too old for passionate love.

When he finally left Boba was bereft, but she picked herself up, yet again, and carried on regardless. He never wrote a line.

This book ends here as the war and the immediate after-war life ended and a new era began. More people, more troubles, more rabbis and even more adventures of the indomitable person I was proud to call my grandmother.

RELIGION

My Epilogue

My life at this time between 1940 and 1950 was full of 'religion', not belief, faith and spirituality, but the bricks, mortar and traditions of religion.

By the time I was ten I knew all the Jewish rules concerning kosher food and the sabbath plus all the Christian stories about John the Baptist, Jesus and the Virgin Mary.

Friday was the big religious day of the week. After Mrs. Turner had fed me a breakfast of probably egg and bacon I would join the rabbi for morning prayers. He knew nothing of what feeding was going on in the front room.

After prayers I would depart for school in time for the morning service in the church. With all the other children I marched into the church, genuflected to the altar and took my seat in the pew.

I liked the church as there was always something at which to stare. My favourite thing was the statue of St. Stephen standing amidst the stones that had killed him. Christianity's first martyr, but I thought he had a nice face and a blue robe.

St. Stephen's is a high church, or was in those days, so there were lots of statues, candles and stained-glass windows.

Father Sheffield took the service in his robes and the altar boys swung the incense holders.

I knew the boys who usually wore shorts and stained jumpers and poked their tongues out at the girls. In church they looked like angels and acted their part proficiently. After church they were as horrible as ever.

I sang the hymns and made the responses and I suppose there was a sermon, but I don't remember listening to the priest. Mostly between the parts of the service I would be whispering to the girl in the next seat.

After school on the Friday when I got home Boba was frying fish and generally getting ready for the Sabbath. My job was to clean the brass candlesticks ready for the candles to be lit when sabbath arrived at sundown.

I also had to lay the sparkling white tablecloth ready for the bread and the wine. Rabbi Baum would take me to the evening service, no statues to look at, just the men shaking in their prayer shawls and chanting the prayers. One thing was the same, I never listened to this sermon either.

When we got home Boba had the meal ready and whoever was living in the house at the time sat at the table. More prayers before the meal, the food and more prayers afterwards. By the end of the day I was sated with prayers, but definitely no better a person.

I suppose I could have a walked on either religious road or none, but Judaism is in my bones and that you cannot shed. When I went to school and church I put on my Christian overcoat which felt quite comfortable, but was quite happy to take it off once at home.

When I had put away childish things I decided that Christianity was too full of an after-life in which I could not believe and orthodox Judaism was religion without too much reality so I have arrived at Reform Judaism. Here I feel mostly comfortable and can be more or less myself.

I tell my rabbi that God lives at the bottom of my garden amongst the rhubarb, cabbages and weeds. Here I can commune with a being that I suppose is there and if not, at least I can think aloud, stamp my feet, think about love and pick the daisies.